NEWCOMER'S
HANDBOOK™
FOR
Washington, DC

NEWCOMER'S HANDBOOK™
FOR
Washington, DC

FIRST BOOKS

P.O. Box 578147
Chicago, IL 60657
773-276-5911
http://www.firstbooks.com

2nd Edition

Newcomer's Handbook® is a registered trademark of First Books, Inc.

Authors: Jeremy L. Milk, Leslie Milk
Publisher and Editor: Jeremy Solomon
Associate Editor: Bernadette Duperron
Contributor: Susan Graage
Cover Design: Art Machine, Inc.
Production: Art Machine, Inc.

Metro transit map is reproduced with the permission of the Washington Metropolitan Area Transit Authority.

ISBN 0-912301-36-8

ISSN 1093-8850

Manufactured in the United States of America

Published by First Books, Inc., P.O. Box 578147, Chicago, IL 60657, 773-276-5911.

7   Introduction

12   Map of Washington DC area neighborhoods

13   Neighborhoods

    14   Metro Transit Map

District of Columbia

    15   Georgetown
    16   Foggy Bottom
    18   Dupont Circle
    19   Adams Morgan
    21   New U
    22   Kalorama
    23   Connecticut Avenue Corridor
    24   Cleveland Park
    26   American University Park
    27   Capitol Hill

Maryland Suburbs

    29   Bethesda/Chevy Chase
    31   Potomac
    32   Rockville
    33   Gaithersburg
    34   Takoma Park
    35   University Park
    36   Laurel
    38   Mitchellville
    38   Columbia
    39   Annapolis

Virginia Suburbs

41	Arlington
43	Rosslyn/Crystal City
44	Ballston
45	Alexandria
46	McClean/Great Falls
47	Reston
48	Loudoun County

51	Apartment and House Hunting
57	Getting Settled
67	Money Matters
73	Helpful Services
77	Child Care
81	Transportation
85	Shopping for the Home
95	Cultural Life
105	Green Spaces
109	Sports and Recreation
119	Places of Worship
127	Volunteering
131	Lodgings
133	A D.C. Year
137	Useful Telephone Numbers
143	Index
149	About the Authors

Welcome to Washington! Washingtonians have heard their city called many things: Hollywood on the Potomac, the puzzle palace, and the capital of the world. In some ways, Washington is all of these. Still Washingtonians think Washington is the most exciting city on earth, and they are not alone. Many of its most strident detractors spent enormous amounts of time and money running for national offices so they'd earn the right to live here.

Those folks with an eye on a Pennsylvania residence or an office under the Capitol dome aren't the only ones coming to Washington. Thousands of America's best and brightest who have no interest — or at least no immediate interest — in the White House or Congress flock to Washington every year. They know that this is where the political action is. You may well be one of them.

What's more, Washington isn't just a government town anymore. Because the National Institutes of Health are here, the Washington area is on the frontier of bio-technology. Because the Pentagon is here, so are the developers of military hardware and software. Because the regulators are here, so are many highly-regulated industries.

Don't worry about being a newcomer — in Washington almost everybody is or was. There are native Washingtonians, of course, but they are greatly outnumbered by people who came here to study or to work and just fell in love with the place. Few Washingtonians have old family or neighborhood ties in the area. Nobody cares who your father is or what social group your mother belongs to. It is easy to make friends and gain acceptance.

Just don't expect Washington to be like any other American city. We are set apart by more than politics, marble monuments, and national museums. Here are some of the things you need to know about Washington right off the bat:

• **Washington isn't one city.** The Washington metropolitan area (referred to in this publication as Washington) is actually a city and two states: the District of Columbia, Northern Virginia, and suburban Maryland. Each jurisdiction has its own rules for everything from recycling to car registration. And although they are very close geographically, they are oceans apart philosophically.

Northern Virginia is more southern, more conservative, and more inclined to act as if the Potomac River was a national boundary. If it weren't for the Washington Redskins, some locals believe that Northern Virginians might secede from the area altogether.

Suburban Maryland is more liberal and more closely tied to the city itself. It is a truism that Marylanders are often city people whose kids have outgrown elementary school. Past the sixth grade DC public schools are so troubled that many parents opt for private schools or a move to the suburbs.

The District of Columbia is hipper, and younger — although close-in suburbs like Arlington, Alexandria, Bethesda, and Chevy Chase now rival DC as young singles abandon the hassles of DC life in tough budget times. DC is also more political. Residents only attained limited self government a few decades ago and they take their local politics seriously. Neighbors often unite to fight over traffic patterns, development, and the placement of homeless shelters.

• **Washington has no ethnic neighborhoods.** Washington's immigrants most often arrive from other American communities — not directly from other countries. And they came one by one, not in masses. As a result, there are no Italian, Irish, or Polish ethnic neighborhoods here. There is a concentration of Latino newcomers in Adams Morgan and Mount Pleasant, and a designated Chinatown in DC. But mostly Washington is a city where hyphenated Americans come to lose their hyphens.

That is not to say that Washington is a totally integrated city. But today lines of demarcation are based on economic status rather than race. Rock Creek Park divides the District racially and economically. The majority of the residents in the District of Columbia east of Rock Creek Park are lower income African Americans. Middle to upper-income residents, both black and white, are concentrated in northwest neighborhoods and the suburbs.

• **Washington is a city of extremes.** The District of Columbia leads the nation in both affluence and infant mortality (the latter because poor women often lack medical care). Generally, the suburbs are either middle class or affluent, but isolated pockets of poverty live cheek-by-jowl with wealthy neighborhoods. And, because Washington lacks an industrial base, blue-collar/lower middle income neighborhoods are a rarity. The neighborhood focus of this book is on areas that make sense for newcomers to settle in, especially in terms of safety.

• **Washington is surrounded by and divided by The Beltway.** The Capital Beltway is a highway that circles the city of Washington. This road is also a state of mind: politicians and pundits talk about "inside the Beltway" as a never-never land where all policy is made by people who never have to deal with the realities of life like buying bread or paying bills. In fact, the federal government has spread into the Washington suburbs so that many "inside the Beltway" bureaucrats are actually working outside the Beltway.

• **Washington is driven.** While Washingtonians are proud of their beautiful subway system, only a minority of Washingtonians rely on public transportation. The subway system is limited. Because it was designed like spokes in a wheel, all radiating out of the city, it is useless for people commuting from one suburb to another. There are buses and a few commuter rails, but most Washingtonians drive to and from work. And they try to live as close to work as possible, making for a city with many nearby residential areas and lots of big houses on small lots.

Be aware, driving in Washington is not without risk as many foreign diplomats who live and drive here are not always required by their home countries to carry automobile insurance. And, If they hit you, they may be protected by diplomatic immunity. Driving is especially hazardous when it snows. Washington still thinks of itself as a southern city and has not mastered the art of snow removal.

Equally risky is parking in the District of Columbia. Parking fines are a major revenue source for the DC government, and Washingtonians believe that cars are ticketed with gleeful abandon.

• **Washingtonians aren't like most other Americans.** Studies by Claritas, a marketing firm that types people by zip codes on the theory that "birds of a feather flock together," indicate that people in the middle to upper income areas of Washington tend to read more books, jog more, play more tennis, drink more scotch, fly more, and take more adult-education courses than people anywhere else in America. Washingtonians are the best educated Americans, and the area has the nation's highest percentage of women in the workforce and two-career couples.

Washingtonians are less likely to bowl, chew tobacco, drink regular cola, and attend Tupperware parties, according to Claritas. Informal observation indicates that Washingtonians have an unnatural obsession with national politics and the Washington Redskins. In *The Washington Post,* news about the Redskins' health often takes precedence over news about a national health care policy.

• **Washington is alphabet city.** In Washington, there are alphabets everywhere — streets, agencies, and companies are known by letters alone. Pierre L'Enfant laid out the city of Washington with numbered streets running North–South and lettered streets running East–West. All addresses begin at the Capitol. This simple grid system should make it impossible to get lost in Washington, except that L'Enfant threw in scenic traffic circles and diagonal avenues named after states to confuse diplomats and tourists. Federal agencies are often known by their initials — the Environmental Protection Agency is the EPA, the Securities and Exchange Commission is the SEC, etc. The local power company is PEPCO for Potomac Electric Power. To add to the alphabet soup, several major private-sector employers are known only by initials — BDM, IBM, PRC.

• **Washington is a world of its own.** Washingtonians tend to dine out more, own more foreign-made products, use more personal computers, travel more, and rank number one among the top 10 metropolitan markets in furniture buying. What does that say about the city — it's educated, affluent, upscale, and so unlike the rest of the country that it will never be a test market. And, if you believe the media, people don't cook much in Washington. Gourmet shops and restaurants sprout up everywhere to serve the dining-out and carrying-out crowd.

• **Washington's crime is concentrated.** Every night, local news stations report on drive-by shootings and gang slayings in Washington. They usually occur in the Northeast and Southeast quadrants of the city. The victims are usually young men from these inner-city neighborhoods. Most Washingtonians who live and work outside these areas of the city do not witness the daily violence firsthand.

The violent crime has made all Washingtonians more cautious — there are some neighborhoods that, if possible, people don't venture into. And fewer people are willing to take a chance on moving into fringe communities like Mount Pleasant, Southwest, Prince George's County inside the Beltway, and parts of Silver Spring, MD and Arlington, VA. Crime is also creeping out of the inner-city into the more affluent parts of the District and suburban neighborhoods.

• **Washington is a green city.** Washington is known for its white marble monuments, but it is also one of the greenest cities in America. Rock Creek Park rambles through the District, and lush green space lines the Potomac on both the Maryland and Virginia sides of the river. Also, there are parks in almost every neighborhood. Many of these national treasures are beautifully maintained by the National Park Service, which plants oceans of daffodils and tulips for your springtime viewing pleasure. (See the "Green Space" chapter for more park information.) Even downtown neighborhoods have tree-lined streets so that you never feel like you're in a concrete jungle. Adding to this feeling of leafy openness is the District's requirement that no building or structure can be taller than the Washington monument — so everywhere in the city you can see the sky.

Neighborhoods

The following neighborhoods are profiled:

DISTRICT OF COLUMBIA

Georgetown

Foggy Bottom

Dupont Circle

Adams Morgan

New U

Kalorama

Connecticut Avenue Corridor

Cleveland Park

American University Park

Capitol Hill

MARYLAND

Bethesda/Chevy Chase

Potomac

Rockville

Gaithersburg

Takoma Park

University Park

Laurel

Mitchellville

Columbia

Annapolis

VIRGINIA

Arlington

Rosslyn/Crystal City

Ballston

Alexandria

McLean/Great Falls

Reston

Loudoun County

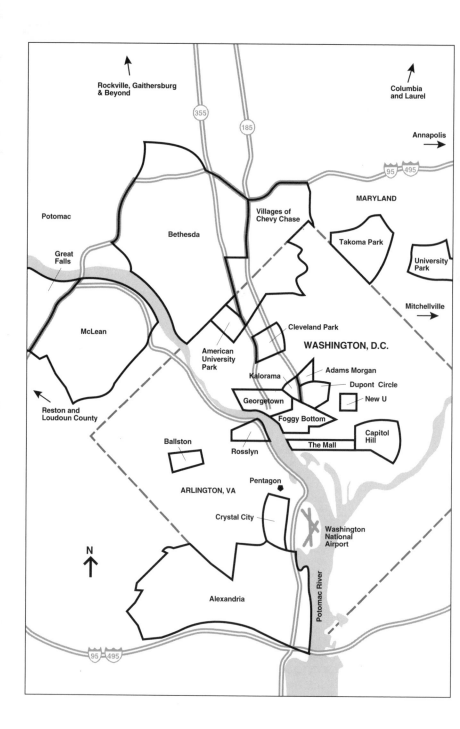

Neighborhoods in the Washington area are known less for their distinctive housing styles or geography and more for the nature of their residents. In workaholic Washington, you can often judge a neighborhood by what workplaces are nearby. Active and retired military gravitate to the Virginia neighborhoods near the Pentagon. Congressional aides house hunt on the Hill. Diplomats live within easy driving distance of Massachusetts Avenue's "embassy row." Most DC police officers commute from Prince George's County and southern Maryland where housing prices in safe neighborhoods are affordable even for those on civil service salaries. Computer specialists set up their homes and homepages along Rockville Pike and Dulles Access corridors. Medical researchers and those on the frontiers of biotechnology tend to live a mere virus away from the National Institutes of Health in Bethesda.

This emphasis on the proximity between home and work makes sense in an area where the car is the most common form of transportation. In addition, many people here work more than a five-day week. Impromptu trips back to the office or lab at night or on weekends are common—there is an unwritten rule in many workplaces: "If you don't come in on Sunday, don't come in on Monday."

The biggest impact on neighborhoods in the past twenty years has been the growth of the subway. Communities like Ballston in Virginia sprung up overnight with the birth of a Metro station. And where there were new apartment complexes, schools, stores, and services soon followed. The lack of neighborhood history is no problem for Washingtonians. There is enough history and character in the city itself. "Metro," as it is known, is such an attractive alternative to clogged commuter routes that some Washingtonians rate proximity to Metro first when they look for housing.

The following neighborhood profiles are written to help you get a feel for each neighborhood. Also included in each profile are details about housing, public transportation, post office locations, hospitals, schools, police, libraries, and cultural resources.

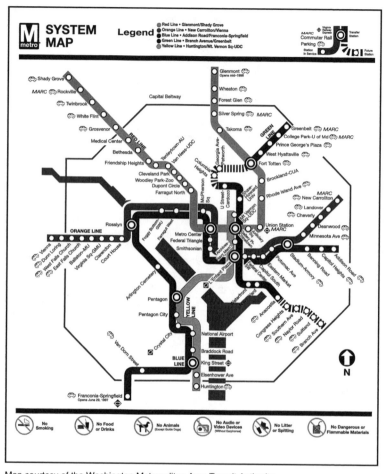

Map courtesy of the Washington Metropolitan Area Transit Authority

DISTRICT OF COLUMBIA

Georgetown

Boundaries: North: Whitehaven Street and Whitehaven Park; **East**: Rock Creek Parkway; **South**: Potomac **West**: Potomac River.

Before upstart colonials dreamed of a nation, let alone a nation's capital, Georgetown was a bustling port on the Potomac River. It was just below the famous Great Falls, and thus the farthest upriver that traders could go. Much of its historic charm remains, and there are even a few cobblestone streets left today.

Georgetowners like to complain that their neighborhood isn't what it used to be when the young Kennedys lived on N Street. But legendary former *Washington Post* editor Ben Bradlee, as well as numerous other power people, still have digs here. Reading the party reports in *The Washington Post*, it would seem that much of the city's permanent hoi polloi break bread here.

Mostly Georgetown consists of beautiful row houses on tree-lined streets with few apartments in sight. Some of the homes are more than 200 years old, and the bear plaques to prove it. Historic preservation rules require that house exteriors be kept intact, but inside most owners have added the comforts of air-conditioning — an absolute necessity during Washington's almost tropical summers. Not all of the houses and apartments in Georgetown are old — some are just designed to look that way. A few years back, Georgetown Visitation Preparatory School sold a parcel of land in this area which was developed into 144 federalist-style townhouses. The list of buyers was a Who's Who of Washington.

At the bottom of Georgetown, right on the river, is the new (by Georgetown standards) **Washington Harbor Complex**. There are apartments here, with some of the finest views in the city, but these residences all run in the high six-figures. Trendy, young Washingtonians crowd the bar at Sequoia on weekends for a wonderful view of the river and each other.

Don't expect any bargains — Georgetown houses are as pricey as they are pedigreed. Georgetown University students seeking rentals must cross the river into Virginia, go uptown, or cram into packed group houses. Many opt for this last choice because the area is so beautiful.

The Georgetown campus also adds to the neighborhood a beautiful leafy greensward, a great library, and tennis courts, not to mention a gothic steeple that towers above.

Twenty years ago, Georgetowners hoped to keep crowds out of their neighborhood by keeping the subway away. But hordes of young locals and tourists still flock to Wisconsin Avenue and M Street every weekend, lured by the bars and clubs that line the crossroads. They also find some of the toniest shops in town — antique stores specializing in French and English furniture, and European boutiques in the glass and brass Georgetown Park Mall. Some residents and shop owners, resigned to the fact that they will always be living in a tourist attraction, are now pushing to get a Metro stop built in their neighborhood — but there is no chance that anything will come of this for years.

Georgetown was plagued by minor street crime a few years ago, but its prominent residents leaned on the city, and the police presence is now obvious, especially on weekends. On a recent Halloween night, the cops outnumbered the costumed celebrants.

Just above Georgetown is **Glover Park**, with lots of group houses, growing families, and restaurants that can't quite manage to pay the Georgetown rent prices down the road. **Foxhall Village**, an award-winning development of English-style houses built in the 1920's, is just west of Georgetown.

Area Code: 202

Zip Codes: 20007, 20037

Post Office: Georgetown Station, 3015 30th Street NW, 202/523-2405.

Police Station: District Station, 3320 Idaho Avenue NW, 202/282-0070.

Emergency Hospital: Georgetown University Medical Center, 3800 Reservoir Road NW, 202/687-2000.

Library: Georgetown Regional Library, Wisconsin Avenue & R Street NW, 202/727-1353.

School District: District of Columbia.

Metro Stop: None.

Cultural Resources: Georgetown University Office of Performing Arts, Leavey Center, 202/687-4081, sponsors countless performances by students and visiting musicians and dancers.

Foggy Bottom

Boundaries: North: Pennsylvania Avenue; **East**: 17th Street; **South**: E Street; **West**: Potomac River.

A stone's throw from the State Department, the World Bank, and George Washington University (GW), Foggy Bottom is home to a diverse mix of row and apartment houses, diplomats, and students. Some of the row houses were built 100 years ago for the workers at the Christian Heurich Brewery, which once stood where the John F. Kennedy Center for the Performing Arts stands today.

Look for one of Washington's most famous addresses, **The Watergate**, in Foggy Bottom. It was here, in one of these circular, white buildings, that the burglary of the Democratic Headquarters occurred. The cover-up led to the resignation of President Richard Nixon. The Watergate is home to former Senator and presidential candidate Bob Dole and his wife Elizabeth, who heads the American Red Cross. Supreme Court Justice Ruth Bader Ginsburg also calls the Watergate home. The complex has condominiums, offices, and the posh Watergate Hotel. The shops at the Watergate include a number of designer boutiques like Gucci and Rive Gauche featuring Yves St. Laurent.

There are countless Foggy Bottom apartment complexes with all of the standard amenities — concierge, rooftop-pool, carpeted hallways. You'll also find more basic housing for tighter budgets. Just be sure to inquire whether a building caters to students — in case you are seeking peace and quiet.

Foggy Bottom borders both Georgetown and the downtown business district, so a host of fine restaurants and clubs are only minutes away. But Foggy Bottom also has its own neighborhood attractions: the jazz club One Step Down and a string of reasonably-priced restaurants and bars catering to GW students.

Like many urban universities, GW is a school without a real campus. However, for neighbors, it does offer lectures and concerts at Lisner Auditorium, good college basketball at the Smith Center, and excellent continuing education programs at night. (See the Higher Education section in the "Cultural Resources" chapter.)

Near Foggy Bottom, along 22nd, 23rd, L, and M Streets, a bunch of luxury condos have gone up within the last few years. The condos here won't offer you great views from their windows, but they offer convenient location, lots of space, and modern trimmings that can't be found elsewhere in this neighborhood.

Area Code: 202

Zip Codes: 20006, 20035, 20036, 20052

Post Office: Watergate Station, 2512 Virginia Avenue NW, 202/965-2730.

Police Station: District Station, 3320 Idaho Avenue NW, 202/282-0070.

Emergency Hospital: George Washington University Medical Center, 901 23rd Street NW, 202/994-1000.

Library: West End Library, 24th & L Streets NW, 202/727-1397.

School District: District of Columbia.

Metro stop: Farragut West, Foggy Bottom (both Blue and Orange lines).

Cultural Resources: The John F. Kennedy Center for the Performing Arts, 202/467-4600, hosts an orchestra, operas, and other shows. George Washington University's Lisner Auditorium, 730 21st Street NW, 202/994-6800, is the location of more than 200 events a year, including concerts, ballets, and lectures.

Dupont Circle

Boundaries: North: T Street; **East**: 17th Street; **South**: M Street; **West**: 22nd Street.

In its heyday in the 1870s, Dupont Circle was the showplace for the mansions of the men who made fortunes in the railroads, mining and publishing. Today, Dupont Circle houses a more eclectic mix of Washingtonians.

This is one District neighborhood where the sidewalks don't roll up at sundown. The apartment houses near Dupont Circle attract singles and DINKs (double income no kids) who love the downtown location and the walk-on-the-wild-side atmosphere.

The neighborhood also welcomes gays and lesbians, which is why many shops here display an inverted pink triangle or rainbow flag in their windows. The Lambda Rising bookstore and several other retailers cater almost exclusively to the gay community. Halloween "drag races" have become such a draw that every year the police close down a wide swath of P Street just for the occasion. (Note: newcomers interested in gay life may want to consult the excellent Washington chapter of George Hobica's *Gay USA*.)

Many Dupont Circle row houses have been converted into apartments of all shapes and sizes, while the elegant old mansions now house embassies and headquarters for various interest organizations. Brewer Christian Heurich's mansion now houses the Columbia Historical Society. Buildings put up within the last 50 years offer your more standard one- and two-bedroom apartments. One-bedroom English basements are particularly popular rentals for couples starting out in the city. Some complain that rents in Dupont Circle are jacked up to artificially high prices because landlords recognize the neighborhood's strong urban appeal, but that doesn't stop people from moving to Dupont Circle in droves.

The high rents have forced many artists out of the area. However R Street, west of Connecticut Avenue, still has a strong concentration of galleries.

The circle itself is a meeting place during the day for bicycle couriers, executives from nearby office buildings, and street people. Around noon, on any given day, all can be seen playing chess on tables along the circle's perimeter. At night many residents avoid the circle's panhandlers and stick to the sidewalks. Dupont Circle boasts great ethnic restaurants, cafes, and alternative stores. More shops in this neighborhood serve cappuccino than in any other neighborhood in the Washington area.

Because of its close proximity to so many stores as well as office buildings, Dupont Circle might just be the only place in the city where having a car is completely unnecessary.

Area Code: 202

Zip Codes: 20005, 20036, 20037

Post Offices (nearest): Farragut Station, 1145 19th Street NW, 202/523-2506; Temple Heights Station, 1921 Florida Avenue NW, 202/232-7613; Twentieth Street Station, 2001 M Street NW, 202/523-2410.

Police Station: District Station, 1624 V Street NW, 202/673-6930.

Emergency Hospital (nearest): George Washington University Medical Center, 901 23rd Street NW, 202/994-1000.

Library (nearest): West End Library, 24th & L Streets NW, 202/727-1397.

School District: District of Columbia.

Metro Stop: Dupont Circle (Red line).

Cultural Resources: The Jewish Community Center of Washington, 16th & Q Streets NW, 202/775-1765, has Theater "J" which presents plays of Jewish interest. The Phillips Collection, 1600 21st Street NW, 202/387-2151, is an art museum that showcases French and American works, and hosts frequent lectures and discussions.

Adams Morgan

Boundaries: North: Euclid Street; **East**: 15th Street; **South**: T Street; **West**: 19th Street.

Transplanted New Yorkers feel right at home in this ethnically-mixed neighborhood. Ethiopian restaurants sit next to French cafes, African-style jewelry stores, and Latino markets. Hispanic newcomers, young people, and adventurous young professionals share the area. Clint Eastwood called this place home in the movie "In the Line of Fire."

Adams Morgan got its name when the principals of the predominantly white Adams School and the predominantly black Morgan School called residents together to improve the neighborhood. That meeting was called "the Adams Morgan Better Neighborhood Conference," and the tolerance it created still characterizes the neighborhood today.

Apartment houses and row houses transformed into apartments comprise the bulk of the housing in the neighborhood, and just about every house has a roof deck. During the eighties, gentrification bloomed on the side streets here, turning almost-abandoned buildings into show-places. Rents are also quite low here, by Washington standards, to a large degree because break-ins are more common and there is a lack of subway access.

Residents swear by the farmers market held every Saturday at the 18th Street-Columbia Road intersection. Farmers come from Pennsylvania, Maryland and Virginia to sell produce from their trucks. Adams Morgan celebrates its own diversity and spirit every September, with a festival that includes tons of exotic cuisines and hours of international musical performances.

Parking is a nightmare in Adams Morgan, particularly on weekends when Washingtonians converge upon 18th Street and Columbia Road's hip neon restaurants and clubs. Many residents know just not to use their cars once they have secured a good spot for the weekend.

One warning about this area: crime in Adams Morgan can be a problem. Local restaurants and clubs do their best to keep the main thoroughfares well-lit and heavily-traveled, but it seems that every weekend street criminals mug pedestrians walking to cars and homes on the area's darker side streets. Still, Adams Morgan is much safer than neighboring **Mount Pleasant** and **Columbia Heights**. These two areas were considered up-and-coming in the late 1980s, but a string of violent crimes and robberies put an end to their brief boomlets.

Area Code: 202

Zip Codes: 20009

Post Offices (nearest): Kalorama Station, 2300 18th Street NW, 202/523-2904; Temple Heights Station, 1921 Florida Avenue NW, 202/232-7613.

Police Station: District Station, 1624 V Street NW, 202/673-6930.

Emergency Hospital (nearest): Howard University Hospital, 2041 Georgia Avenue NW, 202/865-6100.

Library (nearest): Mount Pleasant Library, 16th & Lamont NW, 202/727-1361.

School District: District of Columbia.

Metro Stop: None.

Cultural Resources: District of Columbia Arts Center, 2438 18th Street NW, 202/462-7833, hosts everything from art exhibits to dance performances to poetry readings. GALA Hispanic Theater, 1625 Park Road, NW, 202/234-7174, presents classic Spanish drama and contemporary plays about the Hispanic experience.

New U

Boundaries: North: W Street **East**: 12th Street **South:** S Street
West: 16th Street .

New U is the latest designation for the neighborhood in the area of 14th
and U Streets NW. Previously the New U area was considered a part of
the historic **Shaw** neighborhood, where the homes of well-to-do African-
Americans graced the streets, and restaurants and theaters earned Shaw
the sobriquet of Washington's Harlem. Riots destroyed much of the area
in the 1960's and little restoration or development occurred until the last
decade. Emerging businesses and Gen- Xers, committed to making innovative restaurants, galleries and offbeat stores succeed, make New U a
welcome addition to the somewhat conservative District. Reminiscent of
New York City's East Village, young hipsters in the artistic vanguard coexist with recently arrived Hispanic and Asian immigrants and an established African-American community to give New U a diverse flair.

More affordable than the surrounding areas of Dupont Circle and
Adams Morgan (rents are generally 30-40% less), New U however does
not possess the restored Victorian townhouses and distinguished brown-
stones of those areas. It is a bit more urban and commercial in feel, and
is not as leafy and green as other District neighborhoods—it doesn't contain any parks or areas suitable for dogs. The ever growing phenomenon
of the dollar store and multiple fast food establishments adjoin small
shops offering refinished furniture and used books. There is no major
supermarket within easy walking distance, but there are a number of
neighborhood delis as well as other necessary businesses, from dry
cleaners to a relatively well equipped gym called Results.

New U boasts a number of restaurants well worth the trip, such as
Coppi's (1414 U Street), where thoughtfully topped pizzas and creative
salads can be enjoyed at a leisurely pace with selections from an impressive list of Italian wines. Another local favorite is the legendary Ben's
Chili Bowl (1213 U Street), a regular stopping point for celebrities such
as Bill Cosby and Denzel Washington when visiting the District. Some of
Washington's best alternative music, from Memphis blue-eyed soul to
industrial squall and all musical points in between, can be found at
venues such as State of the Union (1357 U Street) and the Black Cat
(1831 14th Street). With patrons focused on music and conversation,
most clubs in the area are a haven for folks fleeing the "pick-up" mentali-
ty that pervades many other D.C. bars.

U Street does have the advantage of Metro accessibility (the U
Street/Cardozo stop on the Yellow and Green lines) and is home to the
newly constructed Reeves municipal building, which serves as an anchor
for the emerging neighborhood. The not quite gentrified nature of New U
has led many residents to complain of property crime in particular, but for
adventurous and creative idealists on a budget, New U is the Washington neighborhood of choice.

Area Code: 202

Zip Code: 20009

Post Office: T Street Station, 1915 14th Street NW, 202/483-9580.

Police Stations: District Station, 1801 Columbia Road NW, 202/673-6826; District Station, 3031 14th Street NW, 202/673-4331.

Emergency Hospital: Howard University Hospital, 2041 Georgia Avenue NW, 202/865-6100.

Library: Watha T. Daniel Branch, 8th & Rhode Island Avenue NW, 202/727-1228.

School District: District of Columbia.

Metro Stop: U Street-Cardozo (both Yellow and Green lines).

Kalorama

Boundaries: North: Rock Creek Parkway; **East**: 22nd Street; **South**: Massachusetts Avenue; **West**: Massachusetts Avenue.

Stretching from Connecticut Avenue below Calvert Street's Taft Bridge to Massachusetts Avenue, Kalorama is a mix of stately consulates and classic residences. It's the type of neighborhood in which a home with a ballroom is normal. Many homes have beautiful back gardens, and Rock Creek Park, which winds through Kalorama, adds still more greenery.

Many of the apartment houses here date back to before World War I, when no building was complete without maids' quarters. These apartments remain among the most elegant residences in town. They are also some of the most costly. West of Connecticut Avenue, however, there are some more reasonable, less pedigreed condos, many of which are available for rental.

Though this neighborhood has always attracted its share of White House officials, Congressmen, and diplomats (Franklin Roosevelt, Herbert Hoover, and Woodrow Wilson, to name a few), don't expect to see city news makers in the local check-out line. Kalorama does not have many stores within easy walking distance. Depending on where in this neighborhood you live, you might not be too far from the restaurants of either Adams Morgan or Dupont Circle.

Area Code: 202

Zip Codes: 20008, 20009

Post Office: Kalorama Station, 2300 18th Street NW, 202/523-2904.

Police Station: District Station, 3320 Idaho Avenue NW,
202/282-0070.

Emergency Hospital (nearest): George Washington University
Medical Center, 901 23rd Street NW, 202/994-1000.

Library (nearest): Cleveland Park Library, Connecticut Avenue &
Macomb Street NW, 202/727-1345.

School District: District of Columbia.

Metro Stop: Dupont Circle, Woodley Park-Zoo (both Red line).

Connecticut Avenue Corridor

Boundaries: North: Chevy Chase Circle; **East**: Rock Creek Parkway
and Beech Drive; **South**: Taft Bridge; **West**: 34th Street and Reno Road.

Connecticut Avenue from the Taft Bridge to Chevy Chase Circle is one of
the great residential thoroughfares of Washington. The neighborhood
names change as you head northward, from Woodley Park to Cleveland
Park to Van Ness to Chevy Chase, DC. But the essential character of the
area remains: a mix of apartment houses built between the 1920s and
1970s, 1930s row houses broken up into apartments, and small restaurants and stores. The side streets are lined with more of the same, mixed
with large, older, expensive houses, many of which are rented by groups
of friends.

The corridor has an abundance of condominiums as well as rental
apartments. Singles, couples without children, retirees, and diplomats
are attracted to the area for its convenience and Old-World charm.
Smaller homes in this area are affordable for middle-income families.
Buildings here offer spacious rooms and leafy views. They often have a
concierge's desk, and some of the newer buildings have swimming pools
and fitness rooms. These digs, many offering efficiency and "junior one
bedroom" apartments, attract hordes of recent college graduates.

The **Woodley Park** section of the Connecticut corridor has the
widest sidewalks, enabling restaurants to venture outside with their
tables. Sidewalk cafes are still new to Washington, but they have flour-
ished in Woodley Park for years. The National Zoo draws locals as well
as tourists. Until recently, Washington was obsessed with its pair of giant
Pandas, Ling Ling and Sing Sing. Their romantic lives made headlines
every Spring as the city united in a panda pregnancy watch. One of the
pandas died in 1993 and the sympathy cards are still displayed around
the panda house.

Further up Connecticut Avenue, near the Van Ness/UDC Metro stop,
is the University of the District of Columbia (UDC) and the Howard University Law School. A number of embassies and the headquarters of the
International Satellite Organization are directly across from UDC. The

city's public university has no dormitories — students commute to classes — so the neighborhood does not feel like a college town. **Van Ness** has many modern high-rise apartments with underground garages. This neighborhood has only a few good restaurants, but plenty of shops.

There is a small residential section between Connecticut Avenue and Rock Creek Park which is known for beautiful and expensive contemporary houses, some walled almost entirely with glass. The most desirable homes border the park. One of this neighborhood's hidden treasures is the Hillwood Museum of French and Russian art and Japanese gardens, housed in the Merriweather Post mansion.

Area Code: 202

Zip Codes: 20007, 20008, 20009, 20010, 20011, 20015

Post Offices (nearest): Cleveland Park Station, 3430 Connecticut Avenue NW, 202/523-2395; Friendship Station, 4005 Wisconsin Avenue NW, 202/635-5305; Kalorama Station, 2300 18th Street NW, 202/523-2904.

Police Station: District Station, 3320 Idaho Avenue NW, 202/282-0070.

Emergency Hospital (nearest): George Washington University Medical Center, 901 23rd Street NW, 202/994-1000.

Library (nearest): Cleveland Park Library, 3223 Connecticut Avenue NW, 202/727-1345.

School District: District of Columbia.

Metro Stop: Cleveland Park, Van Ness/UDC, and Woodley Park/Zoo (All Red line).

Cultural Resources: The Hillwood Museum, 4155 Linnean Avenue NW, 202/686-5807, holds French and Russian decorative arts and boasts Japanese and English gardens.

Cleveland Park

Boundaries: North: Tilden Street; **East**: Rock Creek Park; **South**: Cathedral Avenue; **West**: Wisconsin Avenue.

Located between Woodley Park and the Van Ness/UDC area is Cleveland Park, which spreads throughout the northern part of the District of Columbia. This neighborhood first attracted residents because it was the high ground — blessed relief from the swampy heat of Washington summers. In fact, Cleveland Park got its name from President Grover Cleveland, who bought a country "cottage" in the area in 1886. Similar "cottages," with their wraparound porches built to catch the cool breezes, still line the streets of Cleveland Park.

Some of the local houses are palatial, but there are also more modest, three-bedroom colonials in this neighborhood. You'll see few driveways in Cleveland Park — instead there are narrow alleys lined with garages behind the houses.

Cleveland Park is home to city policy types, think tank wonks, administration aides, and *Washington Post* publisher Donald Graham. Residents of the this area's zip code, 20009, donated more money to political campaigns than any other zip code, with the exception of one in Beverly Hills and one in Manhattan.

Cleveland Park is also home to area's most prestigious private schools, including the National Cathedral School and St. Alban's School. The area attracts families — some of the District's best public elementary schools are here — and groups of singles. There are many group houses in this neighborhood, especially along Macomb, Newark, and Tilden Streets.

Cleveland Park's historic preservationists have successfully blocked major commercial development in their community — even on Connecticut Avenue. The city's finest big-screen movie theater, The Uptown, still graces Connecticut Avenue in Cleveland Park, and the neighborhood supports a two-block strip of interesting stores and restaurants.

Area Code: 202

Zip Code: 20008

Post Office: Cleveland Park Station, 3430 Connecticut Avenue NW, 202/523-2395.

Police Station: District Station, 3320 Idaho Avenue NW, 202/282-0070.

Emergency Hospital (nearest): George Washington University Medical Center, 901 23rd Street NW, 202/994-1000.

Library: Cleveland Park Library, 3223 Connecticut Avenue NW, 202/727-1345.

School District: District of Columbia.

Metro Stop: Cleveland Park (Red line).

American University Park

Boundaries: North: Western Avenue; **East**: Wisconsin Avenue; **South**: Garfield Street; **West**: Canal Road.

Head North on Wisconsin Avenue or MacArthur Boulevard and you'll find yourself in American University (AU) Park. Here residents enjoy old trees shading embassy-sized houses, townhouses, upscale apartment complexes, and traditional three-bedroom colonials. The atmosphere changes from street to street. Foxhall Road is the home of Rockefeller and ambassadors.

Not everybody in the leafy neighborhood surrounding American University's park-like campus is a multimillionaire or a celebrity. The streets around the university also offer some of the city's best housing buys and rentals. Nice two-bedroom homes with fenced-in yards can be rented for the price of one-bedroom apartments in Dupont Circle — drawing many AU professors and graduate students as well as those looking for the most space for their buck.

A revival of nearby **Tenleytown**, complete with a new Fresh Fields supermarket and Hechinger's hardware store, have AU Park residents glowing about the shopping here.

The area is fairly safe because it has few commercial strips. Even near the university, the Sutton Place shopping center caters to a wine and cheese rather than beer and pretzels crowd. One disadvantage to those living on the MacArthur Boulevard side of AU Park: no Metro stop within walking distance means you have to rely on buses or drive to work.

Area Code: 202

Zip Codes: 20016

Post Office (nearest): Friendship Station, 4005 Wisconsin Avenue NW, 202/635-5305.

Police Station: District Station, 3320 Idaho Avenue NW, 202/282-0070.

Emergency Hospital (nearest): Sibley Hospital, 5255 Loughboro Road NW, 202/537-4080.

Library: Tenley-Friendship Library, Wisconsin Avenue & Albermarle Street NW, 202/727-1389.

School District: District of Columbia.

Metro Stop: Tenleytown (Red line).

Cultural Resources: American University Department of Performing Arts, Kreeger Building, 4400 Massachusetts Avenue NW, 202/885-4320, offers performances by students and professionals.

Capitol Hill

Boundaries: North: H Street; **East**: 8th Street; **South**: Southeast Freeway; **West**: North Capitol Street and South Capitol Street.

A neighborhood of early 20th Century row-houses immediately surrounding the United States Capitol, Capitol Hill is a mix of restored houses tended lovingly by a cross-section of homeowners, including congressional staffers, lobbyists, and journalists, and civil servants. With a racial mix close to 50-50, it very well might be the most balanced section of the city.

Thomas Jefferson once lived here, and even today your next-door neighbor is likely to be a newly elected member of the House. Some Congressmen whose families stayed back home in their districts live together in group houses on "the Hill." Many recent college graduates also find spaces in group homes, where they can get their own rooms at reasonable prices. Very little housing has been built here for decades.

A cautionary note: Capitol Hill residents have a major problem with street crime, and everyone seems to know someone who has been mugged. Residents stay because of the incredible convenience the neighborhood offers to anyone who works on the Hill. The U.S. Capitol Police, in response to several street crimes directed at members of Congress and their staff, have stepped up their patrols of the area immediately surrounding the Capitol, but this change has had little impact beyond a four or five block radius.

Nearby **Union Station** has been transformed from a dilapidated train station into a hip, urban market-place with restaurants, boutiques, and movie theaters, adding a whole new place for nightlife on the Hill. Many residents still prefer the less-glitzy restaurants, bars, and boutiques on Maryland Avenue that have served this neighborhood for decades. It's at places like these that you're likely to bump into the Speaker of the House quaffing a beer on a Tuesday night. On weekends, locals flock to the Eastern Market in for fresh produce, art, and hand-made crafts.

To the west of Capitol Hill, a new neighborhood of luxury buildings and trendy restaurants is emerging. Dubbed "**Penn Quarter**," this near-Hill neighborhood includes **Market Square** and the **Lansburgh** — two pricey buildings featuring high-ceilings, 24-hour concierge and views of the Capitol Dome. Expect to pay dearly for the convenient location, views, and amenities.

Five years ago you wouldn't have wanted to walk through this part of town, but now restaurants and stores are rushing to set up shop here. Penn Quarter is also home to the Shakespeare Theatre. But you're far more likely to see a young Kennedy or two than a young Macbeth in an apartment around here.

Area Code: 202

Zip Codes: 20001, 20002, 20003, 20013

Post Offices: National Capitol Station, 2 Massachusetts Avenue NE, 202/523-2628; Southeast Station, 327 7th Street SE, 202/523-2173.

Police Station: District Station, 415 4th Street SW, 202/727-4655.

Emergency Hospitals: Washington Hospital Center, 110 Irving Street NW, 202/872-6101; Children's National Medical Center, 111 Michigan Avenue NW, 202/884-5000.

Libraries: Library of Congress, 1st Street & Independence Avenue SE, 202/707-5522; Southeast Library, 7th & D Streets SE, 202/727-1377.

School District: District of Columbia.

Metro Stops: Capitol South, Eastern Market (both Blue and Orange lines), Union Station (Red line).

Cultural Resources: Capitol Hill Arts Workshop, 545 9th Street SE, 202/547-6839. Cultural Alliance of Greater Washington, Suite 600, Stables Art Center, 410 8th Street NW, 202/638-2406. Tomorrow's World Art Center, Room 301, 410 8th Street NW, 202/347-3646. The Shakespeare Theater, 450 7th Street NW, 202/393-2700, puts on the Bard's works year-round, often with internationally renowned actors. The Library of Congress, 1st Street & Independence Avenue SE, 202/707-5522, frequently hosts art and photographic exhibits as well as dance performances.

MARYLAND SUBURBS

Bethesda/Chevy Chase

Boundaries: North: Tuckerman Lane **East**: Rock Creek Parkway, Beech Drive, and Connecticut Avenue; Route 270, Tuckerman Lane, Strathmore Avenue, and Knowles Avenue; **South**: Military Road; **West**: MacArthur Boulevard.

These close-in suburbs are known for big houses, small lots, and wall-to-wall over-achievers raising their children to be likewise. Most of the area is devoted to single-family houses, but apartment complexes and strips of townhouses are sprouting up near Metro stops. These range from the luxurious to the spartan. There are always a number of houses available for rent because the owners are often posted to another country but want to hold onto their property here. Bethesda and Chevy Chase have more than their share of high-profile neighbors. The next person in line at Strosnider's Hardware in Bethesda might just be journalist Cokie Roberts. Justice Sandra Day O'Connor, journalists David Brinkley and George F. Will hang their hats in Chevy Chase. The combination of diplomats and the throng of foreign doctors who are here to work at the National Institutes of Health add international flavor.

Old Chevy Chase has stately homes, big trees, and two of the area's oldest and most exclusive country clubs, the Chevy Chase Club and the Columbia Country Club. This is where the old families of Washington, known as "cave-dwellers," play tennis and entertain in rooms that have never been noticeably redecorated. When *Worth* magazine listed the nation's richest neighborhoods, several sections of Chevy Chase ranked high. However, Chevy Chasers are not showy. More beat-up Volvos line the narrow streets here than shiny new Mercedes.

Bethesda has a more varied mix of residents and housing options. Once the sole province of families, Bethesda is a haven for singles and DINKS (double income, no kids) now that the Metro has transformed the downtown areas of Bethesda and Chevy Chase from suburban hamlets into cities, making these areas more attractive to a younger crowd. **Friendship Heights**, the Chevy Chase area around Wisconsin Avenue where Maryland and the District meet, is also known as Gucci Gulch because of the upscale stores and luxury apartments in the area. Some Marylanders whose children have grown up are trading their suburban mansions for condos in Friendship Heights. Many complexes here offer shuttle bus service to the Friendship Heights Metro station along with many other amenities. Two upscale shopping complexes face off on Wisconsin Avenue: Mazza Gallerie has Neiman Marcus and a brand-new Filene's Basement, while Chevy Chase Pavilion boasts the Cheesecake Factory, an informal eatery that is packed at all hours.

Downtown Bethesda has seen similar growth. High-rise office and apartment buildings cluster around the Bethesda Metro stop. Condos and rentals are now available here. Bethesda has also turned into a restaurant heaven. The Woodmont Triangle area is lined with eateries, from Afghani to Vietnamese, from sawdust floors to crystal chandeliers. The safety of the area and the abundant parking attract suburbanites who no longer find any reason to go into downtown DC for fine dining. New brewpubs, billiards parlors, and week night happy hours cater to the younger crowd.

Further out, in North Bethesda, there is a veritable building boom for townhouse- and apartment-seekers. Once again, access to the Metro is a major selling point.

Area Code: 301

Zip Codes: 20813, 20814, 20815, 20816, 20817, 20824, 20825, 20827

Post Offices: Main Branch, 7400 Wisconsin Avenue, Bethesda, 301/941-2664; Arlington Road Station, 7001 Arlington Road, Bethesda, 301/941-2680; Chevy Chase Branch, 5910 Connecticut Avenue, Bethesda, 301/941-2792; Naval Medical Center Branch, 8901 Wisconsin Avenue, Bethesda, 301/941-2786; and West Bethesda Branch, 9601 Seven Locks Road, Bethesda, 301/365-8673.

Police Station: Montgomery County Police Bethesda Station, 7359 Wisconsin Avenue, Bethesda, 301/652-9200.

Emergency Hospitals: Sibley Memorial Hospital, 5255 Loughboro Road NW, 202/537-4080; Suburban Hospital, 8600 Old Georgetown Road, Bethesda, 301/896-3880.

Libraries: Bethesda Library, 7400 Arlington Road, Bethesda, 301/986-4300; Chevy Chase Regional Library, 5625 Connecticut Avenue NW, 202/727-1341; Davis Library, 6400 Democracy Boulevard, Bethesda, 301/897-2200; Little Falls Library, 5501 Massachusetts Avenue, Bethesda, 301/320-4880.

Metro Stops: Bethesda, Friendship Heights, Medical Center, Grosvenor, White Flint (all Red line).

School District: Montgomery County.

Cultural Resources: The Writer's Center, 4508 Walsh Street, Bethesda; 301/654-8664, offers classes for would-be novelists, non-fiction writers, poets, and playwrights; resources for writers; holds frequent readings. Glen Echo Park, 7300 MacArthur Boulevard, Bethesda, 301/320-5331, holds art classes for both children and adults and has a gallery showing students' and instructors' works. Also home of Adventure Theater, which offers children's theater, classes, and workshops. Strathmore Hall Arts Center, 10701 Rockville Pike, Bethesda, 301/530-0540, offers visual arts shows, concerts, and a sculpture park.

Potomac

Boundaries: North: Wooton Parkway; **East**: Seven Locks Road; **South**: Tuckerman Lane; **West**: Potomac River.

Potomac is such a posh address that residents of nearby Rockville often try to get their mailing addresses changed to be a part of it. Potomac has its share of standard cookie-cutter suburban streets, but the area is known for its beautiful golf courses, its white horse-fences (if you have the fence, who needs a horse) and the mini-estates of the doctors, lawyers, and lobbyists who make up Washington's permanent elite.

Former Wonder Woman Linda Carter and her ex-BCCI lawyer husband Robert Altman live here. Perennial presidential hopeful Jack Kemp's sons starred on the football field for local Churchill High School and newsman Ted Koppel still parks his red Mercedes convertible here. Boxer Sugar Ray Leonard rested between bouts in Potomac until his first retirement, at which time he divorced his wife and moved to Hollywood. In the eighties, Potomac boomed. Architects ran amok and million-dollar houses were routinely built on speculation. For a while in the nervous nineties, construction stopped. But the upscale development around Avenel, a tournament-level golf course, has just been completed and houses sold there like high-priced hotcakes.

Good schools, both public and private, are a Potomac hallmark. The area is familyoriented, with plenty of sports teams and activities for children. However, public transportation is virtually non-existent in Potomac — be prepared to carpool the kids, and budget close to an hour for commuting downtown. Many residents swear they can get downtown in thirty minutes, using back roads to reach the Clara Barton parkway, which parallels the Potomac River and the C & O Canal on the Maryland side. But nobody moves to Potomac for quick access to the city.

Potomac Village is really a suburban crossroads rather than an actual place. Residents do their serious shopping and dining in Rockville or Bethesda. One exception is the Normandie Farm Restaurant, which was serving hot popovers and great slabs of roast beef when Potomac was considered countryside. The inn is still popular, particularly for brunch and Sunday dinners. In the fall and winter, there are roaring fires in the fireplaces, and nobody in the kitchen has ever heard of nouvelle cuisine.

Area Code: 301

Zip Codes: 20850, 20854, 20859, 20874, 20878

Post Offices: Cabin John Branch, 7945 MacArthur Boulevard, Potomac, 301/229-6970; Potomac Branch, 10221 River Road, Potomac, 301/983-4670.

Police Station (nearest): Montgomery County Police Bethesda Station, 7359 Wisconsin Avenue, Bethesda, 301/652-9200.

Emergency Hospital (nearest): Suburban Hospital, 8600 Old Georgetown Road, Bethesda, 301/896-3880.

Library: Potomac Library, 10101 Glenolden Drive, Potomac, 301/983-4475.

Metro Stop: None.

School district: Montgomery County.

Cultural Resources: Potomac Community Theater, 301/299-6803, has performances, plays, readings, and children's summer theater camp.

Rockville

Boundaries: North: Warfield Road; **East**: Georgia Avenue; **South**: Montrose Road and Randolph Road; **West**: Wooton Parkway and Seven Locks Road.

The city of Rockville has had a number of reversals of fortune since its early life as a sleepy town along the Georgetown Pike several decades ago. The white clapboard houses were surrounded by ugly tracts and three-story garden apartment complexes, and the Montgomery County government built one ugly building after another in the seventies. Rockville built a windowless, enclosed mall right in the middle of town that attracted few businesses and even fewer patrons. Meanwhile, traffic on Rockville Pike, the main shopping artery of the western county, slowed to a crawl as the number of people driving up and down "the Pike" exceeded its capacity.

In the past few years, however, Rockville has been trying to make a comeback. Affordable rents are attracting young people, and the widening of Route 270 has helped the traffic problem. "Happy Hours" abound on the Pike, a sign that not everyone in the suburbs is a mom in a minivan.

Twenty years ago, the area past Rockville was filled with dairy farms and corn fields. Now the cows have been crowded out by subdivisions of townhouses and single-family homes in Gaithersburg, **Darnestown**, and beyond. The Route 270 corridor from Bethesda to Frederick is lined with new housing and strip malls — all the features that mark suburban sprawl. For some, Rockville Pike is a shopper's paradise, with stores selling just about everything that a Washington consumer might need or want.

Area Code: 301

Zip Codes: 20847, 20848, 20849, 20850, 20851, 20852, 20853

Post Offices: Courthouse Station, 2 West Montgomery Avenue,

Rockville, 301/838-2922; Pike Station, 143 Rollins Avenue, Rockville, 301/231-5973; Rockville Main Branch, 500 N. Washington Street, Rockville, 301 /838-2900; Twinbrook Station, 2001 Viers Mill Road, Rockville, 301/838-2933.

Police Station: Montgomery County Police Rockville Station, 1451 Seven Locks Road, Rockville, 301/279-1591.

Emergency Hospital: Shady Grove Adventist Hospital, 9901 Medical Center Drive, Rockville, 301/279-6000.

Library: Rockville Library, 99 Maryland Avenue, Rockville, 301/217-3800.

Metro Stops: Rockville, Twinbrook, White Flint (all Red line).

School district: Montgomery County.

Cultural Resources: Rockville Arts Place, 100 East Middle Lane, 301/309-6900, is a nonprofit visual arts center with education programs for children and adults, a resident artist program, and gallery shows. Round House Theater, 12210 Bushey Drive, 301/933-9530, is a professional theater company that performs both classic and contemporary plays. It is also a theater school.

Gaithersburg

Boundaries: North: Goshen Road; **East:** Georgia Avenue;
South: Shady Grove Road; **West:** Route 28, Darnestown Road

People willing to go further out from the District are able to get more house and land for their money. There is also a greater variety of housing options — including subsidized housing and single-family homes of every architectural style from colonial to contemporary. Gaithersburg residents commuting to jobs in downtown DC can get to work faster than many living in the more immediate suburbs because of Metro and the MARC trains that run from Gaithersburg to Union Station. In addition, the growth of the high-tech industrial complexes all along Route 270 and in the Gaithersburg area means that people who live here can often find work within minutes of their home.

Montgomery Village is part of Gaithersburg, but it deserves a mention all its own. This planned community is smaller than the "new towns" of Reston and Columbia, both of which are mentioned later in this chapter, but Montgomery Village offers many of the same features: a mix of apartments, townhouses, and single-family houses in various styles, recreational facilities, and shopping.

Another stand-out development in Gaithersburg is **Kentlands**. Planners here abandoned wide open spaces for the intimacy of eighteenth and nineteenth century villages. The community is still being developed, but so far residents love the neighborliness encouraged by narrow streets and village greens.

Area Code: 301

Zip Codes: 20854,20855, 20856, 20877, 20878, 20879, 20880, 20882, 20884, 20885, 20886, 20898

Post Offices: Diamond Farms Branch, 23 First Field Road, Gaithersburg, 301/208-3708; Gaithersburg Branch, 21 S. Summit Avenue, Gaithersburg, 301/208-3700; Montgomery Village Branch, 10079 Stedwick Rd., Gaithersburg, 301/208-3715.

Police Stations: Montgomery County Police Germantown-Gaithersburg Station, 20000 Aircraft Drive, Germantown, 301/840-2650.

Emergency Hospital: Montgomery General Hospital, 18101 Prince Philip Drive, Olney, 301/774-8900.

Libraries: Damascus Library, 9701 Main Street, Damascus, 301/253-5100; Gaithersburg Library, 18330 Montgomery Village Avenue, Gaithersburg, 301/840-2515;

Metro Stop: Shady Grove (Red line).

School district: Montgomery County.

Cultural Resources: Olney Theatre Center for the Arts, 2001 Olney-Sandy Spring Road, Olney, 301/924-4485, an old summer theater that has been converted to house a year-round Equity theater, touring company, experimental theater, and theater school.

Takoma Park

Boundaries: North: Piney Branch Road; **East**: 14th Avenue and New Hampshire Avenue; **South**: Carroll Avenue; **West**: Georgia Avenue.

Welcome to Washington's nuclear-free zone, where sixties kids can always find Birkenstock sandals, beads, multi-grain breads, and like-minded neighbors. The town government once debated banning backyard barbecues because of pollution.

Hilly, winding streets, lush greenery, and old-fashioned architecture give this area a small town feeling. Individuality is also a hallmark of Takoma Park. Brick Cape Cods share the narrow, winding streets with clapboard Victorians and fifties split-levels. Houses and apartments coexist peacefully. The hilly terrain makes lawns and placement of houses idiosyncratic. You'll quickly notice that not every house faces the front.

The Seventh Day Adventist Church has a college, a hospital and other facilities in Takoma Park, all in a charming campus setting that only enhances the neighborhood. "Downtown" Takoma Park has a smattering of unique shops including a gallery featuring only Honduran art, a natural-fiber clothing store, and the House of Musical Traditions, which sells folk instruments from all over the world as well as recordings and sheet music. Somebody is usually strumming a tune in a corner of the crowded shop. From April to November, Takoma Park has its own farmers market which is limited to producers — no middlemen.

Takoma Park is one of Washington's melting pots, both ethnically and economically. CNN anchor Bernard Shaw is a long-time Takoma Park resident. Town pride and citizen involvement have kept the streets safe — but street crime has become more of a problem lately.

Area Code: 301

Zip Codes: 20911, 20912

Post Office: Takoma Park Post Office, 6909 Laurel Avenue, Takoma Park, 301/270-4392.

Police Station (nearest): Montgomery County Police Silver Spring Station, 801 Sligo Avenue, Silver Spring, 301/565-7744.

Emergency Hospital: Washington Adventist Hospital, 7600 Carroll Avenue, Takoma Park, 301/891-7600.

Library: 101 Philadelphia Avenue, Takoma Park, 301/270-1717.

Metro Stop: Takoma (Red Line).

School district: Montgomery County.

University Park

Boundaries: North: University of Maryland; **East**: Baltimore Boulevard; **South**: East-West Highway; **West**: Adelphi Road.

University Park is a completely residential community of some 950 families located just south of the College Park campus of the University of Maryland — often viewed as the Bethesda/Chevy Chase of Prince George's County. The town attracts professors from the university and those seeking the Montgomery County experience in PG County.

University Park is one of the Washington area's best housing buys. Its large and stately homes would go for $50,000 more in Montgomery County. There is no commercial development permitted in this town. Standard 1920's and 1930's red-brick colonials are the norm, but there are more than a few exceptions, including a section of 1950's ramblers.

The area is rich in recreational facilities, parks, and tennis courts reserved "for University Park residents only." Several town-wide annual events, including a May Garden Tour and July Fourth Picnic, add to the small town flavor. The theaters, lectures, and playing fields of the university are right next door.

University Park Elementary school continues to produce the county's highest math and reading scores on standardized tests, and most parents are active in the PTA.

Residents are determined to keep the town's community feel, and they spent years preparing for the addition of Metro to the area. They say they won't let traffic or pollution become a problem. And they've already changed a few local streets to deter drivers from taking short-cuts through the neighborhood.

Area Code: 301

Zip Codes: 20781, 20782

Post Offices: College Park Post Office, 9591 Baltimore Avenue, College Park, 301/345-1714; Riverdale Post Office, 6411 Baltimore Avenue, Riverdale, 301/699-8859.

Police Stations: Prince George's County Police District I Station, 5000 Rhode Island Avenue, Hyattsville, 301/699-2630; University Park Police, 6724 Baltimore Boulevard, Hyattsville, 301/277-0050.

Emergency Hospital (nearest): Washington Adventist Hospital, 7600 Carroll Avenue, Takoma Park, 301/891-7600.

Libraries (nearest): Beltsville Library, 4319 Sellman Road, Beltsville, 301/937-0294; Hyattsville Library, 6530 Adelphi Road, Hyattsville, 301/779-9330.

Metro Stop (nearest): College Park-University of Maryland (Green line).

School District: Prince George's County.

Cultural Resources: The University of Maryland at College Park offers both visual and performing arts programs.

Laurel

Boundaries: North: Guilford Road; **East**: Guilford Road and Baltimore Washington (BWI) Parkway; **South**: Laurel Fort Meade Road; **West**: Interstate 95.

Most of this Prince George's County suburb looks like all other suburbs: one townhouse sub-division after another, and rows of cookie cutter houses built to shelter all the people who came to Washington after the second world war.

But old Laurel is a gem with hundred-year-old wood-frame Victorian houses. Many have been carefully restored with pine floors and leaded-glass windows. They run under $300,000, depending on the extent of the renovation.

The houses aren't the only appeal of Laurel. This is a real neighborhood with a baby sitting co-op, a Fourth of July cookout, and a hardware store within walking distance. The town is also conveniently located for those families in which one person works in Washington and another works in Baltimore.

Not far from Laurel is the town of **Savage**, where an old sailcloth mill has been converted into an arts center. Here you'll find paintings, pottery, antiques, collectibles, and foot-long kosher hot dogs. Note: this sleepy hamlet is the proposed site of the new Washington Redskins stadium and such a structure would bring much more traffic and development to the area.

Area Codes: 301, 410

Zip Codes: 20707, 20708, 20709, 20723, 20724, 20725, 20726

Post Offices: 324 Main Street, 301/498-1400; 12625 Laurel-Bowie Road, Laurel, 301/490-1818.

Police Station: Prince George's County Police District II Station, 601 S.W. Crain Highway, Bowie, 301/249-7100.

Emergency Hospital: Laurel Regional Hospital, 7100 Van Dusen Road, Laurel, 301/725-4300.

Libraries: Laurel-Howard County Library, 9525 Durness Lane, Laurel, 410/880-5975, Laurel-Prince George's County Library, 507 7th Street, Laurel, 301/779-6790.

Metro Stop: None.

School district: Prince George's County.

Cultural Resources: Laurel Oratorio Society, 301/490-7504, is a professional-level community chorus that works with local schools and presents two or three concerts annually. Montpelier Cultural Arts Center, 12826 Laurel-Bowie Road, Laurel, 301/953-1993, is the county's first multifaceted arts center, houses galleries, classes in visual and literary arts, and performances including the Montpelier Jazz Series, Montpelier Chamber Dance Series, and Montpelier Music Recital Competition.

Mitchellville

Boundaries: North: Northview Drive and Mitchellville Road; **East:** Route 301; **South:** Central Avenue; **West:** Collington Branch Stream Valley Park.

This upscale enclave in Prince George's County boasts spacious houses that look like embassies on bigger lots for less money than you'd pay in next door Montgomery County. One of the most undeveloped areas of Prince George's County, you'll still find woodland, country roads, and an occasional neighbor using goats to trim the front lawn. You can expect Mitchellville to be one of the hot spots in town over the next decade or so.

The area also has the county's highest average household income and has attracted many African-American professionals. Black Entertainment Television just located it's first theme restaurant, BET Sound Stage, near here.

Area Code: 301

Zip Code: 20717

Post Office: 6710 Laurel-Bowie Road, Bowie, 301/464-0707.

Police Station: Prince George's County Police District II Station, 601 S.W. Crain Highway, Bowie, 301/249-7100.

Emergency Hospital: Bowie Health Center, 15001 Health Center Drive, Bowie, 301/262-5511.

Library: Bowie County Library, 15210 Annapolis Road, Bowie, 301/262-7000.

Transportation: 15 minutes from the New Carrollton Metro stop.

School District: Howard County, Prince George's County.

Columbia

Boundaries: North: Clarksville Pike and Waterloo Road; **East:** Interstate 95 and Waterloo Road; **South**: Scaggsville Road and Interstate 95; **West**: Clarksville Pike and Scaggsville Road.

Columbia sits next to Interstate 95, midway between Washington and Baltimore, and its residents work in both cities. A planned community developed by James Rouse, Columbia has nine villages with their own schools, shopping centers, and recreational facilities. Eighty percent of the children in Columbia walk to school.

More and more Columbia residents work as well as live here. There are more than 2,000 businesses in Columbia itself, and the Route 29 corridor near Columbia has become a high-tech mecca.

Recreation reigns supreme in Columbia. Five thousand of its 14,000-acres are devoted to parkland. There are 3 lakes, 128 playground "tot lots" for small children, 60 miles of biking and running trails, 25 racquetball courts, 20 softball fields, a golf course, 19 outdoor swimming pools, 3 indoor swimming pools, a horse center, an ice-skating rink, a roller-skating rink, a bowling center, and a game preserve.

Columbia's developers committed themselves to racial and economic diversity, so you'll find low-cost housing as well as top-of-the-line lakefront homes in this planned community. What you won't find is individuality. Every element, from street signs to the color of your front door, must fit the architectural code. It makes for the kind of uniformity that would make an iconoclast long to go out and paint his or her whole house orange!

Area Code: 410

Zip Codes: 21044, 21045, 21046

Post Office: Columbia Main Post Office, 6801 Oak Hall Lane, Columbia, 410/381-0121.

Police Stations: Howard County Police, 3410 Court House Drive, Columbia, 410/313-3200.

Emergency Hospital: Howard County General Hospital, 5755 Cedar Lane, Columbia, 410/740-7890.

Library: Columbia Library, 10375 Little Patuxent Parkway, Columbia, 410/313-7890.

Metro Stop: None.

School District: Howard County.

Cultural Resources: Columbia Festival, 410/715-3044, is an annual festival for both visual and performing arts. Merriweather Post Pavilion, 301/982-1800, hosts outdoor concerts by internationally known performing artists.

Annapolis

Boundaries: North: Severn River; **East**: Chesapeake Bay; **South**: South River and Chesapeake Bay; **West**: Route 97.

Annapolis was originally a big port city, but with the rise of Baltimore it took on a small-town status. That status is part of its appeal today. A famous town for strolling, it retains the feel of a colonial fishing village, complete with period homes, cobblestone streets, and oysters on the half-shell available on every corner. And, like Georgetown and Virginia's Alexandria, Annapolis residents work hard to maintain the town's colonial feel.

At the same time, though, Annapolis has suburbanized, and it now offers the same chain stores that can be found at every other mall in the Washington area.

Chesapeake Bay boaters and sailors endure the hour-long commute to downtown DC for the joy of living on the water, and doing so in one of the most beautiful historic towns in the country. Housing prices are much lower than in the city of Washington, and waterfront property on the Chesapeake and Severn Rivers is available. If you ever saw Jack Ryan's home in the movie "Patriot Games," you've seen what kind of beautiful homes are present.

Annapolis is the state capital of Maryland, and during the legislative session, the coffee shops are filled with delegates. Annapolis is also home to the U.S. Naval Academy, and on weekends the town is inundated with midshipmen, known around town as "Middies," out in their dress whites. Many Annapolis families "adopt" Naval Academy freshman, providing them with the family atmosphere and support that some new middies need.

St. John's College, one of the nation's few schools to concentrate on "Great Books" rather than standard academic subjects, is also located in the heart of Annapolis.

Area Code: 410

Zip Codes: 21401, 21402, 21403, 21404

Post Office: Annapolis Junction Post Office, 10964 Guilford Road, Annapolis Junction, 301/725-4403.

Police Station: Annapolis City Police, 199 Taylor Avenue, Annapolis, 410/268-9000.

Emergency Hospital: Anne Arundel Medical Center, 64 Franklin Street, Annapolis, 410/267-1000.

Library: Annapolis Area Library, 1410 West Street, Annapolis, 410/222-1750.

Metro Stop: None.

School district: Anne Arundel County school district.

Cultural Resources: Annapolis Chorale, 801 Chase Street, 410/263-1909, offers chorale, chamber orchestra, and youth chorus.

Annapolis Opera, 801 Chase Street, 410/267-8135, presents two
opera performances a year and six-cosponsored musicals, and it
holds an annual vocal competition. Annapolis Symphony Orchestra,
801 Chase Street, 410/269-1132, is a professional orchestra.

VIRGINIA SUBURBS

Arlington

Boundaries: North: Williamsburg Boulevard and N. Glebe Road; **East**:
Potomac River; **South**: Route 395 and Route 7; **West**: Route 7.

Arlington is the chunk of Virginia originally slated to be part of the diamond that formed the District of Columbia. When the District planners
gave the land back to Virginia, they created close-in suburbs with some
of the prettiest views of the nation's capitol. Most of Washington's signature photographs showing the Capitol dome, the Lincoln Memorial, the
Washington Monument, and the Jefferson Memorial are shot from the
Virginia side of the Potomac River, in Arlington.

The most famous national landmarks in Arlington are military — the
Pentagon, Arlington National Cemetery, and the Iwo Jima Memorial.
Along with Fort Myer, they form a military complex that attracts a large
number of active and retired military personnel to the nearby Virginia
suburbs. Former Chairman of the Joint Chiefs of Staff Colin Powell lived
here during his Washington tours of duty. He has since retired and
moved upriver.

Arlington is historical and stately. Its old, established neighborhoods
with solid, brick colonial houses are home to Supreme Court Justices,
journalists, and Senators. Between 1900 and 1910, there were 70 subdivisions recorded in Arlington County, creating a wealth of housing stock
in traditional styles.

Young families have long flocked to **Fairlington**, a community of
spacious three-story "garden apartments." Asian newcomers streaming
into Washington from Vietnam, Cambodia, and Thailand after the Vietnam War gravitated to Arlington, perhaps because many of them had ties
to the military. As they prospered, many moved to outlying Virginia suburbs. But the plethora of Asian restaurants and Pho noodle houses are
an Arlington hallmark, and the community has the most services to assist
newcomers. "Little Vietnam" is as close as Washington comes to an
authentic ethnic neighborhood.

The liberal attitude of Arlington has also attracted a substantial gay
and lesbian community. Also, more and more young professionals, driven from DC by the high housing prices, are also discovering Arlington.
The cafes in the Shirlington complex offer late night dining — a rarity in
Washington — and nightlife is beginning to flourish here. Arlington County also provides a unique facility for performing artists — the Gunston
Arts Center. Gunston has two theaters, and costume and scenery shops
which support a number of local classes and performing companies for

children and adults. On any given day, there are opera singers rehearsing in one room and tiny tappers practicing next door. Arlington also boasts the kind of mom and pop neighborhood stores that are fast disappearing elsewhere. For example, locals swear by the Heidelberg Pastry Shoppe on N. Culpepper Street where you can get bratwurst as well as bread and marzipan treats at holiday times.

Area Code: 703

Zip Codes: 22202, 22203, 22204, 22205, 22207, 22210, 22215, 22216

Post Offices: Main Office, 3118 N. Washington Boulevard, Arlington, 703/525-4838; Central Station, 235 N. Glebe Road, Arlington, 703/525-4170; North Station, 2200 George Mason Drive, Arlington, 703/536-1828.

Police Stations: Arlington City Police, 1425 Courthouse Road, Arlington, 703/558-2222.

Emergency Hospitals: Arlington Columbia Hospital, 1701 N. George Mason Drive, Arlington, 703/558-5000; Northern Virginia Doctors Hospital, 601 S. Carlin Springs Road, Arlington, 703/578-2080.

Libraries: Central Library, 1015 N. Quincy Street, Arlington, 703/358-5990; Aurora Hills, 735 S. 18th Street South, Arlington, 703/358-5715; Cherrydale, 2190 North Military Road, Arlington, 703/358-6330; Columbia Pike, 816 South Walter Reed Drive, Arlington, 703/358-5710; Glencarlyn, 300 South Kensington Street, Arlington, 703/358-6548; Shirlington, 2700 South Arlington Mill Drive, Arlington, 703/358-6545; Westover, 1800 North Lexington Street, Arlington, 703/358-5260.

Metro Stops: Ballston, Clarendon, Court House, Virginia Square, East Falls Church (all Orange line).

School District: Arlington County.

Cultural Resources: Gunston Arts Center, 2700 South Lang Street, Arlington, 703/358-6960, houses a number of arts groups, including the Arlington Dance Theatre, Teatro de Luna, Horizons Theater, and the Arlington Players. The Arlington Symphony Orchestra, 703/528-1817, uses Bishop O'Connell High School for performances. The Arlington Center for Dance, 3808 Wilson Boulevard, Arlington, 703/522-2414, offers classes in ballet, modern, jazz, and tap for children and adults. Signature Theatre, 3806 South Four Mile Run,

Arlington, 703/820-9771, is an award-winning professional theater producing five plays a season. Stephen Sondheim thought so much of Signature that the famous playwright gave them the rights to produce the first off-Broadway run of "Passion."

Rosslyn/Crystal City

Boundaries: North: Spout Run Parkway; **East**: Potomac River and National Airport; **South**: Interstate 95; **West**: Shirley Highway and Colonial Village.

Welcome to Washington's concrete jungle. Metro's first Virginia stations were in Arlington County, specifically in the high-rise boom-towns of Rosslyn and Crystal City. This area, directly across the river from Georgetown, near both the Pentagon and National Airport, had obvious allure for defense contractors and others doing business with the federal government. Residential developers followed the contractors. Talk-show host Larry King is one of many notables who live in these high-rise neighborhoods.

Rosslyn is convenient, but it lacks charm, and as a result never managed to attract the large number of residents that developers had hoped for. But a revival is now underway, led by the 1997 opening of The Newseum, an interactive museum about news and the media, and Freedom Park, a memorial to journalists killed in the line of duty, featuring outdoor sculptures and icons from modern news history. Several townhouse developments are also sprouting up on the edges of Rosslyn.

Crystal City, in the shadow of National Airport, is one of the largest multi-use complexes in the country. The 39 golden brick buildings have 6,100 rental and condominium apartments, three hotels, two health centers, a movie theater, 22 restaurants, 130 stores, and 21 office buildings. Crystal City has its fans and its detractors. This is no place for lovers of greenery or individuality. On the other hand, you can get everything from a swim to a shave to a shower gift to a subway ride without ever stepping outside. A network of tunnels connects the buildings and leads directly into the Crystal City Metro stop.

Area Code: 703

Zip Codes: 22202, 22209

Post Offices: Crystal City Post Office, 1735 Jefferson Davis Highway, Crystal City, 703/413-9267; Rosslyn Station, 1101 Wilson Boulevard, Rosslyn, 703/525-4336.

Police Station: Arlington City Police, 1425 Courthouse Road, Arlington, 703/558-2222.

Emergency Hospitals (nearest): George Washington University Medical Center, 901 23rd Street NW, 202/994-1000.

Libraries (nearest): Central Library, 1015 N. Quincy Street, Arlington, 703/358-5990, Aurora Hills Branch, 735 S.18th Street, Arlington, 703/358-5715.

Metro Stop: Crystal City (Blue and Orange lines), Rosslyn (Blue and Orange line).

School District: Arlington County.

Cultural Resources: The Newseum, 1101 Wilson Boulevard, Arlington, 888/639-7386, is a museum dedicated to the history and innovations of news broadcasting and news gathering, featuring a vast array of hands-on exhibits.

Ballston

Boundaries: North: W. Washington Boulevard; **East**: Quincy Street; **South**: N. Glebe Road; **West**: N. Glebe Road.

Ballston is a baby brother to Crystal City and Rosslyn, with smaller buildings and more green space. Housing stock consists of a small pocket of apartment complexes which has attracted a large number of residents seeking new, amenity-rich apartments and easy access to the city by car or subway. Convenient, yes. But don't look here for fine architecture or great views.

Also, most people don't stay in Ballston for more than a few years — it's fine when you're single, or a couple, but this neighborhood doesn't have as much to offer children as neighboring Arlington or Alexandria.

Area Code: 703

Zip Codes: 22201, 22203, 22207

Post Office (nearest): Central Station, 235 N. Glebe Road, Arlington, 703/525-4170.

Police Station: Arlington City Police, 1425 Courthouse Road, Arlington, 703/558-2222.

Emergency Hospital (nearest): Arlington Columbia Hospital, 1701 N. George Mason Drive, Arlington, 703/558-5000.

Library (nearest): Central Library, 1015 N. Quincy Street, Arlington, 703/358-5990.

School District: Arlington County.

Metro Stop: Ballston (Orange line).

Alexandria

Boundaries: North: Shirley Highway and S. Glebe Road;
East: Potomac River; **South**: Interstate 95; **West**: Quaker Lane.

George Washington shopped the streets of Old Town Alexandria, and the historic district is so well maintained that you still expect a booted and bewigged George to stride around the cobblestoned corner. Every other house on these narrow, tree-lined streets seems to bear a bronze historical plaque and woe unto any resident who tries to alter an authentic facade. Owning a house in Old Town is not for the shallow of pocket. Even the new brick townhouses on the outskirts of Old Town run in the high six-figure range.

Just outside of Old Town are a number of new and established apartment complexes which cater to singles and young couples. What they lack in architectural excitement, these complexes make up for with convenience. Most are on major bus lines and some offer shuttle service to Metro. These complexes also offer swimming pools, tennis courts, workout rooms, party rooms, and lots of social activities.

One standout complex is **Parkfairfax**, a group of three-story garden apartments built after World War II. Former Presidents Richard Nixon and Gerald Ford brought their young families here to live. Many of the units in the complex are really two-story townhouses. Parkfairfax has been converted from rentals to condominiums.

Between Alexandria and Mount Vernon, you'll find some of the prettiest residential neighborhoods in the area. Expect mostly center hall Colonial style homes, as this is the old dominion, with a wide price range. One exception is the contemporary community of **Hollin Hills** — nearly five hundred low-slung houses built into the hills. Cited by Life magazine in 1951 as among the "best houses for under $15,000," a quarter of the original owners are still in residence. Today the houses, most of which have been expanded over the years, sell for $240,000 to $400,000.

Whereas neighboring Arlington attracts twenty-somethings at night, Old Town Alexandria is the center of nightlife for people over thirty on the Virginia side of the River. Restaurants, bistros, and bars line the streets. The Dandy, the riverboat restaurant that plies the Potomac, is docked here. You'll find everything from haute cuisine to Ben and Jerry's ice cream. Old Town also houses fine galleries, boutiques, and specialty stores. The Torpedo Factory is a weekend mecca for art lovers. The factory has been converted into studios for painters, sculptors, weavers, goldsmiths, and other artists.

How safe is Alexandria? Its housing projects have seen their share of drug- and gang-related violence, and its major high school, T.C. Williams, has all the problems of many inner-city high schools. However, the Alexandria city government is strong, and committed community leaders work hard on social issues, especially crime related issues. There are no signs of Alexandrians leaving town in fear.

Area Code: 703

Zip Codes: 22301, 22302, 22303, 22304, 22305, 22307, 22308, 22309, 22310, 22311, 22312, 22313, 22314, 22320

Post Offices: Community Branch, 7676 Richmond Highway, Route One, Alexandria, 703/765-4251; Jefferson Manor Branch, 5834-C N. Kings Highway, Alexandria, 703/960-4440; Olde Towne Station, 1100 Wythe Street, Alexandria, 703/549-2620; Potomac Station, 1908 Mount Vernon Avenue, Alexandria, 703/549-2854.

Police Stations: Alexandria Police, 2003 Mill Road, Alexandria, 703/838-4444.

Emergency Hospitals: Alexandria Hospital, 4320 Seminary Road, Alexandria, 703/504-3000.

Libraries: Main Headquarters, 717 Queen Street, Alexandria, 703/838-4555; Ellen Coolidge Burke Branch, 4701 Seminary Road, Alexandria, 703/370-6050; James M. Duncan Jr. Branch, 2501 Commonwealth Avenue, Alexandria, 703/838-4566; Lloyd House, 220 N. Washington Street, Alexandria, 703/838-4577.

School District: Alexandria County.

Metro Stops: Braddock Road, King Street (both Blue and Yellow lines).

McLean/Great Falls

Boundaries: North: Potomac River; **East**: Potomac River; **South**: Old Dominion Drive; **West**: Washington Dulles Access Road.

McLean is the southernmost corner of Northern Virginia — in attitude, not in latitude. Architecture and clothing styles tend to be traditional. A well-known dry cleaner in McLean has a waiting list — in old Virginia, people like things to last. Nearby Great Falls is the equivalent of Maryland's Potomac — except that here the horse fences often hold real horses.

This area of the Potomac has been attracting tourists since Captain John Smith came up from Jamestown in 1608 to look for gold and a northwest passage to the Pacific Ocean. River views are prized, and the natural beauty of the area has been preserved. Great Falls National Park offers river views, hiking, and even challenging rock-climbing. Roads wind to accommodate the terrain — a bonus for beauty but a hazard for winter driving. Residents here could not imagine leveling the land to build better roads as they sometimes do in nearby communities.

McLean and Great Falls are home to much of Washington's elite. In fact, this is a neighborhood with so many heavy hitters that you can almost get a congressional quorum at the Great Falls garbage dump on a Saturday morning.

In terms of housing, you are more likely to find an estate with a guest house than an affordable apartment in this neck of the woods. There are a few luxury townhouse communities and some $200,000 single-family houses considered bargains here. Most homes are priced in the high six-figures and upward.

McLean is just down the road from Washington's biggest shopping mall, Tysons Corner Center. Directly across Chain Bridge Road from Tysons is the Galleria, also known as Tysons II. Across from Tyson's on its Leesburg Pike side is Fairfax Square, a small complex with big price tags. Tiffany and Company, Fendi, Hermes, Gucci, and Louis Vuitton have stores here. Window-shopping is wonderful, as is the pasta at Primi Piatti, a suburban off-shoot of one of DC's best Italian restaurants.

Area Code: 703

Zip Codes: 22101, 22102, 22103, 22043, 22066, 22182

Post Offices: Great Falls Post Office, 748 Walker Road, Great Falls, 703/759-2885; West McLean Branch, 1544 Springhill Road, McLean, 703/356-3522.

Police Stations: McLean District Station, 1437 Balls Hill Road, McLean, 703/556-7750.

Emergency Hospitals (nearest): Columbia Dominion Hospital, 2960 Sleepy Hollow Road, Falls Church, 703/538-2872.

Libraries: Dolly Madison Library, 1244 Oak Ridge Avenue, McLean, 703/356-0770; Great Falls Library, 9818-A Georgetown Pike, Great Falls, 703/759-4750.

School District: Fairfax County.

Metro Stop: None.

Reston

Boundaries: North: Leesburg Pike and Sunrise Valley Drive; **East**: Hunter Mill Road; **South**: Lawyers Road; **West**: Centreville Road.

A Harvard-educated New Yorker named Robert E. Simon Jr. came up with the idea for Reston in the 1960s — he even created the name of the town from his initials. He pictured a multi-use community where residents could live, learn, work, play, and shop without ever leaving their neighborhood. Simon envisioned Reston as a town of seven villages, with 10,000 residents in each.

Reston was not an immediate success. Located in the Virginia countryside near Dulles Airport, the town seemed remote from Washington. Today, the Dulles access road makes commuting easier for those who don't work in the Reston area. But Northern Virginia has developed and moved out to meet Reston, so few Restonites need to go downtown unless they want to.

Recreation is almost a religion in Reston, centered around it's man-made lakes, playing fields, jogging trails, and recreation centers. There is a wide range of housing options available for those who wish to buy or rent.

Like some communities in the DC area, Reston has found snow removal challenging, so on those rare days of significant snowfall, be prepared to hunker it out here in Reston.

Area Code: 703

Zip Codes: 22090, 22091, 22094

Post Office: Reston Post Office, 11110 Sunset Hill Road, Reston, 703/437-6677.

Police Station: Reston District Station, 12000 Bowman Towne Drive, Reston, 703/478-0904.

Emergency Hospitals: Inova, 11901 Baron Cameron Avenue, Reston, 703/471-0175; Reston Hospital Center, 1850 Town Center Parkway, Reston, 703/689-9037.

Library: Reston Regional Library, 11925 Bowman Towne Drive, Reston, 703/689-2700.

School District: Fairfax County.

Metro Stop: None.

Further afield: Loudoun County

Boundaries: North: the Potomac River; **East:** the Potomac River, Dulles Airport; **South:** Route 50, Route 705; **West:** West Virginia state line.

Welcome to hunt county! Loudoun County has more horses per capita than any county in Virginia, and has been known for its rolling hills and rural character. But thanks to new roads and the ever-growing housing needs of Washington workers, Loudoun is now the fastest growing county in the state. You can buy a four-bedroom, two-and-a-half bath house with a two-car garage and a quarter-acre lot here for about $230,000. And the Dulles Greenway has cut commuting time — you can go from the heart of Loudoun county to the Mall without encountering a single stop light. Or dash across the border to Point of Rocks, Maryland and take a MARC train for $5.25 and you'll be in Union Station in 73 minutes.

Loudoun offers a delightful mix of the old and the new. Historic towns like Leesburg and Middleburg are now ringed with acres of new houses. There are still families who've been in the area since the 1700s and poker games that have had the same players for thirty years. But newcomers are changing the landscape and everywhere you look in Loudoun there is construction for schools, libraries, and shopping centers. The area is having its growing pains, as services sometimes lag behind the population boom and old timers complain about "paving paradise," but few areas offer as much in both housing and green space.

History buffs will have a field day here. Historic plantation houses, country inns, and antique shops abound. There is even a ferry that's been running between Maryland and Virginia since 1826. And civil war reenactments frequently take place on weekends.

I n the 1980s, real estate was a hotter topic than politics at Washington gatherings. House prices were rising so fast that all you had to do was buy a house and sit back and count your profits. But by the early 90s, the property party was over. Housing prices have rebounded now, but no longer can you be assured that any house, anywhere is a good investment.

As in other metropolitan areas, as the economy goes, so goes the housing market. The big difference is that Washington used to be recession-proof. That is past history. As the federal government downsized – both in real terms and in dominance of the local economy – Washington lost its protection from recession. But this is still the nation's capital and that fact alone means the housing market doesn't stay depressed for long.

Where should you look for a house. The big question is city or suburbs. The District of Columbia has had more than its share of trouble in recent years. But *The Washington Post* reports that, "despite collapsing roads, deteriorating schools, and insolvent municipal finances more houses and condominiums were sold in the District in 1996 than in any year since the early 1990s." Real estate experts observe that most buyers are young married couples without children, empty nesters, older couples, and families who can afford private-school tuition.

For all its faults, what lures people to DC is location, location, location. Transportation is a breeze and the beauty of the city's parks and historic sites are right in your backyard.

Things to watch out for:

- **Airport noise.** Washington's National Airport is only 15 minutes from downtown – very convenient for Congressmen racing home on weekends but very hard on the ears of a lot of residents. Noise-abatement restrictions keep big planes from taking off and landing at night. You have to visit a neighborhood several times at different hours to really know if you'll be in the National flight plan. Western Virginia suburbs face some of the same problems from Dulles International Airport.
- **Termites.** Washington's temperate climate makes it termite heaven. Termite inspections are required before purchase. It's good advice

to go along on termite inspections to make sure a property is checked thoroughly and to talk to the inspector about any potential problems.

- **Traffic.** Washingtonians drive to work. When major thoroughfares get crowded or are under construction – a constant condition – commuters take to the residential streets. The speed bumps that are now ubiquitous in many neighborhoods are supposed to discourage commuters, or at least slow them down. But many a new home buyer has discovered that a quiet street they saw on a weekend of house hunting has turned into a speedway on Monday morning.
- **Transients.** How stable is the neighborhood? You want neighbors who have roots in the community, who care about the area. Washington is known as a transient town, but some communities have long-time residents who keep community spirit alive.

Renting Versus Buying

Should you rent or buy? The answer is easy if you're a cabinet secretary or a power broker. You pick the house and get out your calculator. Experts say that for a $1 million-house you can expect to pay rent of $4,500 to $6,000 a month. A $1.5 million-house will rent for $6,500 to $7,500 monthly. At that price, it's smarter to buy than to rent.

For those of us on more restricted budgets, the rent versus buy question may be more complicated. Buying provides long-term savings. But many new Washingtonians have come to town on a weekend, bought a house or apartment, and later discovered that they had purchased more than they had bargained for. Sometimes it is wiser to rent first and get to know the area before you make a major investment in a house. One-year leases are common and will give you the time to decide where in the metropolitan area you want to put down some permanent roots.

Washington offers a good selection of rental houses as well as apartments. Some are owned by local families as investments while others are owned by diplomatic and military families who don't want to leave their permanent residences empty while they are posted overseas.

Whether renting or buying in the area, you should be forewarned: there are rarely fabulous deals in the nation's capital. Rent control is limited to a few pockets in the area, and there are no factory lofts waiting to be converted into low-cost show places. Still, you will have little difficulty finding a home in any style or size. As for apartment hunters, what you'll find in the District are row houses converted into apartments, pre-war apartment houses, and newer buildings with more amenities and less charm. In the suburbs, you'll find both high-rise and low-rise complexes.

Newspaper Classified Advertising

The classifieds provide long lists of homes and apartments for sale or rent. Here's a list of the newspapers you will want to check:

- The **Sunday *Washington Post* Real Estate Section** is one of the most comprehensive listings of real estate in the Washington area.
- The ***Washington Times* Friday Home Guide** beats the Post by two days, but the listings are not as comprehensive.
- The ***Washington City Paper*** prints weekly lists of housing to share, housing for rent, and housing for sale, as well as commercial spaces available. While the paper covers the whole area, its classifieds list is best for people seeking to rent inside the District. The *City Paper* comes out on Thursdays.
- ***Roll Call*** is one of the best places to look for rentals if you want to live on or near Capitol Hill. The paper comes out twice a week, on Mondays and Thursdays.

Apartment & Home Guides

Several large real estate companies, developers, and private businesses put together local apartment shopper's and home buyer's guides. These publications include pictures and prices of homes, often organized by neighborhood, as well as real estate advice. Such booklets and magazines are free, and can be found in supermarkets, drug stores, and outside of most Metro stations. Some of the guides focus on certain regions, such as Northern Virginia or Prince George's County, so if you know where you want to live, you might want to go to that area for the housing guides.

On-line Resources

Computer users can surf the world wide web for local homes or apartments available for sale or rental. In addition to ***The Washington Post***'s classifieds listings on-line (**http://www.washingtonpost.com**), the following web sites allow users to search their databases according to desired location, price, and features. The sites offer pictures and contact information. Much like their printed cousins, the on-line guides are produced by real estate companies, developers, and private businesses.

- **http://www.aptguides.com** offers a listing of area apartments for rent.
- **http://www.aptsforrent.com** lists area apartments for rent, including temporary, furnished housing.
- **http://www.harmonhomes.com** includes detailed information about homes for sale in Maryland and Virginia.
- **http://www.treb.com** specializes in sales of single family homes.
- The **Fannie Mae Foundation** also maintains a web-site about buying and financing a home, at **www.homebuyingguide.org**.

Real Estate Brokers

If you're not satisfied with the ads and lists, or want guidance from someone who knows the area and will act as your advocate, you might want to use a real estate broker. Real estate brokers are agents who will represent you, the buyer. What's more, some real estate brokers won't cost you a cent, as they receive a cut of the selling agent's commission. Most agencies will act as real estate brokers. Below is a list of the local biggies. Most offices are independently owned and operated. We've tried to give the numbers of offices that either serve the whole Washington area or can put you in touch with a local office.

- **Century 21**, 800/338-4541 or 301/330-5900
- **Long & Foster**, 301/441-8101 or 703/359-1500
- **Weichert**, 301/718-4111 or 703/739-3100

Old School and Hometown Connections

Word-of-mouth is still one of the best sources for apartments and houses. Get in touch with old college friends or hometown friends as soon as you know you are coming to Washington, and ask them to keep their eyes and ears open. They won't be surprised to hear from you – in a transient town like Washington, where so few people have extended families, calling on previous connections is common. These sources are especially good for finding a place in a group home, because these vacancies are not always advertised.

Corporate Ties

If you've been transferred from the headquarters in Phoenix, or just moved here to take a new job, your employer might be able to help you out. Some employers will recommend a real estate agent, while others will put you up while you look for a place to call home.

Direct Action

There is no law against hitting the pavement and searching for the right home. If you see a building that you like, go talk to the concierge, manager, or whoever owns the building. And if you see a home for sale, pop right in or call the real estate agency selling it and set up a private showing.

Apartment Finding Services

A few companies offer free assistance to newcomers searching for rental apartments. The companies work with and earn commissions from property management companies. They have lists of places in the District, Maryland, and Virginia, and they can show you color videos or photographs and floor plans of the apartments you find appealing. Here are a few companies to call:

- **Apartment Locators**, 301/585-7368
- **Apartment Search**, 800/989-FREE

Roommate Referral Services

Having a roommate means sharing the kitchen and the living room, and often the bathroom; but it also cuts your rent substantially and makes sure that you're not alone in the big city. If you are looking for others to live with but can't seem to find the right people, have no fear – a number of businesses will help you find a decent roommate, for a small fee. Here's a short list of some area referral services:

- **Roommate Finders Service**, Laurel, 301/805-0100.
- **Roommates Preferred**, 904 Pennsylvania Avenue SE, 202/547-4666.

Extra Information for Renters

Leases

The lease is a legally-binding contract that outlines the landlord's obligations as owner as well as your obligations as a tenant. It goes without saying that you should read your lease carefully before signing it.

The lease should state your name and address as well as the name and address of the landlord. It should state the first and last dates of contracted occupancy, the monthly rent, and where the rent is to be paid. It will also contain any specifics that the landlord chooses to add, be it banning pets, requiring lawn maintenance, or prohibiting sub-letting. Do not sign the lease until you are satisfied with all of the terms stipulated in the lease. And don't wait until after signing a lease to discuss a security system or extermination of pests.

Many newcomers want short leases because they intend to buy homes or apartments once they are acclimated to the area. One-year leases are common in Washington and many can be extended on a month-to-month basis. It pays to inquire about this before signing a multi-year agreement.

All landlords are not the loving and considerate people that we'd like them to be, so be sure to walk through the house or apartment with the landlord to make a written record of any damage that existed before you moved in. This way you will not be held financially or legally responsible for this pre-existing damage.

Security Deposits

Just about every landlord will require a security deposit before allowing you to move into your new apartment or home. This security deposit is usually the equivalent of one or two months rent, and will be returned to you with interest when you have moved out and the landlord has determined that you caused no extraordinary damage to the place.

Rent Control

Rent control is just about unheard of in the Washington area. As a result, most landlords negotiate one-year leases and raise rent annually. There are a few communities, like Takoma Park, which mandate rent stabilization to ensure fair rent practices; however this is the exception to the rule.

Landlord Problems

If you have any problems with your landlord, and cannot work out an amicable solution, here are some organizations that will either assist you or provide detailed information about your rights as a tenant:

- **Alexandria Landlord Tenant Relations Office**, 703/838-4545
- **Arlington County Citizen & Consumer Affairs**, 703/358-3260
- **District Department of Housing Division of Contracts & Compliance**, 202/535-1566
- **Fairfax Department of Consumer Affairs**, 703/222-8435
- **Montgomery County Landlord Tenant Affairs Office**, 301/217-3660
- **Prince George's County Department of Housing**, 301/883-5530

Insurance

Whether you choose to rent or buy, you'll certainly want to insure your property. Though well east of the Midwest's "tornado alley," the Washington area is hit by a few small twisters every year. And there will always be small floods, fires, and other disasters, natural and unnatural.

Renters insurance is relatively cheap, since you need only protect your possessions, not the property in which you reside. Homeowners insurance is more expensive, but the cost far outweighs the risk of being without it.

Some of the major national insurance companies have franchises in Washington, so you will have no difficulty finding an agent in your neighborhood. You can also call the companies' toll free numbers to get local referrals. You might also contact **Insurance Information Institute** at 202/833-1580.

- **Liberty Mutual Insurance**, 800/746-7421
- **Prudential Insurance**, 800/530-5035
- **State Farm Insurance**, 888/531-0033

N ow that you've found the home of your dreams, or at least one that you can kick back and relax in on those rare occasions that the President doesn't need your advice, you've got to arrange for connection of utilities. Getting settled also requires registering cars, registering to vote, and all that other tedious stuff that needs to be done in order to fully settle into a new community.

Electricity

The Washington area is served by two electric companies. Both offer a number of special deals for those customers with energy-efficient homes or special needs, such as persons with severe disabilities. They also provide coupons for reduced prices on energy-efficient light bulbs and heaters. Contact your electric company for additional information.

There are no hook up fees for electricity, and you can expect the power to be turned on almost immediately after you request it.

District and Maryland residents call **Potomac Electric Power Company (PEPCO)** at 202/833-7500 for service. Virginia residents call **Virginia Power** at 703/934-9660 for service.

Gas

For a period in the seventies, the Washington area had a moratorium on the extension of gas lines. That is why you may well have an all-electric home or apartment and you can skip this section. If your home does use gas, either in the kitchen or for heating throughout, call **Washington Gas** at 703/750-1000 to request service anywhere in the metropolitan area. As with electricity, renters should expect to pay their own gas bills, though there are exceptions to this rule.

If your home is already equipped for gas, there is no hook up fee; however if you wish to convert an existing electric home into a gas home, be prepared to pay dearly for the change. In some neighborhoods, Washington Gas will only convert your home to gas if a certain number of neighbors also agree to make the switch.

Also, before doing any building or digging in your yard, call **"Ms. Utility" Locating Service** at 800/257-7777 to get gas lines marked.

Phone Service

Bell Atlantic Telephone is the local Baby Bell that provides telephone service to all Washingtonians, though residents in the District, Maryland, and Virginia each have their own respective Bell Atlantic offices to deal with.

The phone company does not offer phones, though it does offer services including Caller ID, Call Forwarding, Call Waiting, Speed Calling, Three-Way Calling, and Voice Mail at additional charges. Combination packages of these services are available. These services are explained in detail in the front section of local phone books, and will also be explained by a customer service representative when phone service is requested.

To get phone service installed or disconnected, District residents call 202/346-1000, Maryland residents call 301/954-6260 and Virginia residents call 703/876-7000. When you order service, you will also have the opportunity to choose your long-distance carrier.

Be aware that the Washington area is going through the same area code issues being faced by the rest of the nation. At this point there are no new area code changes in the works for the District or northern Virginia. In Maryland, however, beginning in 1998 there will be two new area codes added; 443 to the 410 area, and 240 to the 301 area. To further complicate matters, it is always necessary to dial ten digits, even when making local calls (area code plus the number, do not dial a "1").

Driver's Licenses/Vehicle Registration

Few tasks can be more time-consuming and frustrating than dealing with the DMV. However, local governments are attempting to speed the process. For example, Maryland has created several shopping center "Express" offices to speed license renewals, and "Full Service" offices are open one Saturday morning each month. When in doubt about what to bring, call for information before you arrive at a DMV office. Nothing is more annoying than waiting in line for an hour only to learn that you need different identification or some additional document.

District residents can call the DMV at 202/727-6680 for information about driver's licenses and motor registration. New residents must convert licenses and registration within 30 days or face fines. The DMV is located in the District Municipal Center, 301 C Street NW. If you have an out-of-state or foreign driver's license, you can convert it into a District license at the Municipal Center, Room 1157, Window 7. You must bring your old license, take a written test, take an eye test, and pay a fee. If you don't have a driver's license, you must take the tests in order to get a learner's permit, then schedule a road test by calling 202/727-6580. You can register your car in the same room. You must bring your title, inspection papers indicating that the vehicle passed an emissions test, and signed insurance papers from an insurance company licensed to conduct business in the

District. It will cost you for the registration and the plates. There's also an excise tax on each vehicle's book value, 6 percent for those weighing under 3,500 pounds, and 7 percent for those over 3,500 pounds.

Maryland residents have an MVA (Motor Vehicles Administration) instead of a DMV, though the bureaucracy is the same. MVA's are located throughout the area, so you'll most likely only have to wait in line for an hour or so, not a whole day. Montgomery County and Prince George's County residents call 301/948-3177 for license and registration information. New residents must convert licenses and registration within 30 days or face fines. If you have an out-of-state or foreign driver's license, you can convert it into a Maryland license at any Full Service MVA office. You must bring your old license, birth certificate, and social security card, take an eye test, and pay a fee. In some cases you'll have to take either a written or road test. If you don't have a driver's license, you must take the vision and written tests in order to get a learner's permit, then take a road test at a later date. While you're working on the driver's license, you can register your car at the same full service office. You must bring your title, inspection papers indicating that the vehicle passed an emissions test, and signed insurance papers from an insurance company licensed to conduct business in Maryland. Again, it will cost you for the registration and the plates. There's also a 5% excise tax on each vehicle's book value.

Virginia residents can call their DMV at 703/761-4655 for information about driver's licenses and motor registration. New residents must convert licenses and registration within 30 days or face fines. The Virginia DMV has offices located throughout the area, so call for the location nearest your home. If you have an out-of-state or foreign driver's license, you can convert it into a Virginia license at any DMV office. You must bring your old license, birth certificate, and social security card, take an eye test, pay a fee, which varies according to your age, and in some cases take either a written or road test. If you don't have a driver's license, you must take the tests in order to get a learner's permit, then take a road test at a later date. While you're working on the driver's license, you can register your car at the same place. You must bring your title and signed insurance papers from an insurance company licensed to conduct business in Virginia. Most areas also require emissions inspection before granting a Virginia title, so check with the DMV or ask at your neighborhood gas station. You'll have to pay for the registration and new license. There's also an excise tax on each vehicle's book value. The tax varies by jurisdiction and township, usually between 4 and 6 percent.

Parking Laws

Washington might just be the only city in the world that pays its bills with revenues from parking tickets. The $70 plus million per year that the District pulls in on parking tickets is the only reason the city has yet to formally declare bankruptcy, and city officials know it. Often parking officials will wait by a car with only a few minutes on the meter, seeming to relish the opportunity to ticket just one more car.

Maryland and Virginia residents shouldn't think that their out-of-state tags will save them from the city's ever-present wrath — half of the tickets written go right onto the windshields of cars from Maryland and Virginia.

The fury over the meter mania has captured the attention of the DC government. District officials are discussing ways to increase the number of city parking spaces. They are also talking about making parking regulation signs easier to understand. But these changes have been under discussion for years, with no noticeable progress.

In the meantime, Maryland and Virginia governments have joined the foray, and they too are ticketing as much as possible. So read every parking sign carefully, and when in doubt, don't park there.

If you get a parking ticket, you can dispute it by following the instructions on the back of the ticket. Maryland and Virginia parking officials are willing to nullify a ticket that should not have been issued in the first place, while District officials will rarely let you off the hook.

And whatever you do, don't just tear up or ignore parking tickets — parking enforcement offices keep lists of cars that have outstanding parking tickets, and if they find your car, they will put the dreaded "boot" (a locking device), on one of your tires. You won't be going anywhere once you've been "booted."

Television

Can't bear to go another day without C-SPAN? No problem. Several cable companies serve the Washington area. Programming and channels vary slightly between the companies, though each offers basic cable service, and at an additional charge, premium channels. They also offer pay-per-view movies and specials. Parents can request special cable boxes that prevent children from watching certain channels. For installation and service, DC residents call District Cablevision at 202/635-5100; Montgomery County residents call Cable TV Montgomery at 301/424-4400; Prince George's County residents call Jones Communications at 301/499-1980; Alexandria residents call Jones Communications at 703/823-3000; Arlington County residents call Cable TV Arlington at 703/841-7700; and Fairfax County residents call Media General at 703/378-8411.

Of course, you won't need cable to watch the Redskins or "Friends." Here's a list of the national and local TV networks in the area:

Channel 4	WRC/NBC
Channel 5	WTTG/FOX
Channel 7	WJLA/ABC
Channel 9	WUSA/CBS
Channel 20	WDCA/Independent
Channel 22	WMPT/PBS
Channel 26	WETA/PBS
Channel 32	WHMM/PBS
Channel 50	WFTY/WB

Daily TV program listings are printed in both *The Washington Post* and *The Washington Times*, in addition to several local newspapers and weekly magazines like *TV Guide*.

Radio

For those trips around the Beltway, or those rare occasions when you can't find a thing to watch on the tube, you'll want to know what's on the airwaves. Washington has no true Top 40 station, but just about everything else is available. Here's a partial list of the AM radio stations broadcasting in the area:

570 AM	WTEM/Sports
630 AM	WMAL/News & Talk, Sports
730 AM	WCPT/CNN News
980 AM	WWRC/Talk
1050 AM	WKDL/Children's
1390 AM	WMZQ/Country
1500 AM	WTOP/News & Sports
1600 AM	WINX/Oldies.

Here's a list of the big FM stations:

88.5 FM	WAMU/News & Talk & Music (National Public Radio)
90.9 FM	WETA/Classical & Cultural
93.9 FM	WKYS/R&B
94.7 FM	WLTT/Light Rock
95.5 FM	WPGC/R&B
96.3 FM	WHUR/R&B,
97.1 FM	WASH/Light Rock
98.7 FM	WMZQ/Country
99.1 FM	WHFS/Rock
99.5 FM	WGNY/Light Rock
101.1 FM	WWDC (DC101)/Rock
102.3 FM	WMMJ/Light Rock
103.5 FM	WGMS/Classical
104.1 FM	WXTR (Z104)/Dance
105.9 FM	WCXR/Classic Rock
106.7 FM	WJFK/Talk & Jazz
107.3 FM	WRQX/Light Rock.

Voter Registration

Each local jurisdiction has its own board of elections, and most will gladly mail voter registration forms to your new home. Others will tell you where you can find the forms, at such places as public libraries and courthouses. To get in touch with your local board of elections, Alexandria residents call 703/838-4050, Arlington County residents call 703/358-3456, District residents call 202/727-2525, Fairfax County residents call

703/222-0776, Montgomery County residents call 301/217-8683, and Prince George's County residents call 301/627-2814.

Passport Services

The U.S. Passport Office is located at 1111 19th Street NW. This is the only passport office in the area, and as a result it is often quite crowded. Some passport services can be done through your local branch of the U.S. Postal Service, so call the Passport Office at 202/647-0518 for additional information. Passport applications and information can also be found at the U.S. State Department's Bureau of Consular Affairs' homepage, at http://travel.state.gov.

The 19th Street office issues both new passports and renewals. If you've never had a passport before, you'll need proof of citizenship in the form of a birth certificate or naturalization papers, a driver's license or other proof of identity with a photograph, two passport photos, and $65 for adults or $40 for minors. For those renewing a passport, you'll need two passport photos, your old passport, and $55. The process usually takes three to four weeks; three-day emergency service is available for an additional $30.

Recycling

Recycling is becoming mandatory in most of the Washington area. Local governments provide residents with recycling bins, and most neighborhoods have their recyclables picked up weekly. Budget problems in the District have led to several halts of the recycling program, but it appears that it will continue in the long-run.

What gets recycled and when varies throughout the area, so residents should call their local recycling information office for specifics. Following is a list of those phone numbers by area: Alexandria, 703/751-5872; Arlington County, 703/358-6570; District, 202/727-5856; Fairfax County, 703/324-5052; Montgomery County, 301/217-2410; and Prince George's County, 301/883-5963.

Newspaper Subscriptions

You'll probably want to know what's going on in the city, and you'll definitely need something to read while riding Metro. Washington is not a city with news-stands on every corner, though there are coin-operated newspaper boxes at major downtown intersections, Metro stops, and suburban supermarkets.

It is hard to imagine life in Washington without *The Washington Post*. It has the highest market penetration of any metropolitan paper. Conservative readers find relief from what they perceive as *The Post's* leftist leanings by reading *The Washington Times*. Washington is also home to the colorful national newspaper, *The USA Today*. To subscribe to one of these papers, call: *The Washington Post*, 202/334-6100, and

The Washington Times, 202/636-3333. You can call *The USA Today* at 800/872-0001.

For more local information — particularly about your neighborhood — look at some of these other local publications which provide useful information about schools, sports, and neighborhood issues:

- *Gazette* & *Journal* **Newspapers.** These companies write exclusively about what's going on in the suburbs. They offer detailed coverage of high school sports and yard sales.
- *Roll Call* & *The Hill.* These publications are full of Congressional on-goings and local Capitol Hill events. *The Hill* is free and is available in newspaper boxes located near many area Metro stations.
- *Washington Blade.* The largest publication geared towards the gay and lesbian population of the city.
- *Washington City Paper.* This free weekly rivals the *Post* and *Times* as a guide to local cultural events and anything new and hip.
- *Washingtonian Magazine.* The magazine of upscale, educated Washington, this monthly covers power brokers, restaurants, and vacation spots, helpful services, and the latest town gossip.

Pet Laws & Services

The District, Maryland, and Virginia all have leash laws in effect. There are no scoop laws, however you should be considerate of those in your community. Licensing of pets varies from one city and county to another, so ask your vet about specific local requirements, or call the following agencies with animal related questions; in DC residents can call The **District of Columbia Animal Shelter** 202/576-6664, Prince George's County residents call the **Prince George's County Animal Control**, 301/499-8300, in Montgomery County call the **Montgomery County Animal Control** 301/279-1823, or the **Montgomery County Animal Shelter**, 301/217-6999, and, serving Arlington County, D.C., and Fairfax County is the **Animal Welfare League of Arlington**, 703 931-9241.

Unlike some other areas, Washington boasts no official dog parks. And the police — especially the U.S. Park Police, with jurisdiction of national parks and all the monuments — have been known to issue tickets to owners whose dogs are running free in area parks. Still, the police seem to look the other way when it comes to unleashed pets in Battery-Kemble Park in Spring Valley, Lincoln Park in Capitol Hill, and Meridian Hill Park in Northwest, DC.

For a good vet, you might be best off asking your neighbors. Owners of ferrets, falcons, chinchillas, and other rare species can find help at the **Exotic Pet Clinic**, 7297 Commerce Street, Springfield, 703/451-3414. And the **Washington Animal Medical Center** (71 Oglethorp Street NW, 202/726-2556) is the East Coast's only full-service veterinary hospital exclusively for low-income pet owners.

Washington Consumers' Checkbook rates area kennels. You can get their latest guide by contacting the staff at 202/347-7283.

If you trust your little Spot or Fifi at home, and simply need someone to feed or walk him or her while you're away, the following services are available:

- **Alexandria Pet Sitting**, 703/823-9225
- **Pets N Plants**, 703/848-0700
- **Sit-A-Pet Inc.**
  Arlington & Fairfax Counties, 703/243-3311
  District, 202/362-8900
  Montgomery County, 301/424-7100
- **Tender Loving Cat Care**, 301/258-7745

On-line Services

The personal computer and all its lingo, from surfing to downloading to e-mail and on-line chatting, has permeated the daily lives of Washington residents. The DC area, mainly the Maryland and Virginia suburbs along the Dulles Airport route, is also home to high-tech software and computer consulting firms, many of which cater to the federal government. With such high tech immersion it should come as no surprise that you'll have no problem getting connected locally.

The Washington Post's on-line information service, www.washingtonpost.com, is especially useful for newcomers seeking employment. America Online's Digital City offers locals the latest information on clubs, bars, and restaurants.

If you wish to get a dedicated data or ISDN line, District residents call 202/346-1000, Maryland residents call 301/954-6260 and Virginia residents call 703/876-7000.

Local On-line Services

Below are the names and numbers of several reliable local internet service providers, all of which provide their customers with instructions, software, and technical support:

- **Digital Express**, 888/203-4439
- **Erols Internet Service**, 800/376-5772
- **InfiNet**, 800/849-7214
- **Potomac Internet**, 202/331-8989
- **US Net**, 301/572-5926

National On-line Services

It seems that all the national services have gone to flat rates with unlimited services, for about $20 a month. But the industry is evolving by the minute, and with customers increasingly getting busy signals, change is definitely on the horizon. So call the national services to find out about their latest information and packages.

- **America Online**, 800/827-6364
- **AT&T WorldNet**, 800/967-5363
- **Compuserve**, 800/848-8199
- **Delphi**, 800/695-4005
- **Internet MCI**, 800/550-0927
- **Microsoft Network**, 800/426-9400
- **MindSpring Enterprises**, 800/719-4332
- **Prodigy**, 800/776-3449
- **Sprint Internet Passport**, 800/359-3900

E ven in this age of electronic money transfers, you'll need to establish ties with a local bank as soon as you have a permanent address in the Washington area. Our three jurisdictions can make this a little bit complicated — if you open a bank account at a bank in Maryland, you might not be able to make deposits in the same bank's ATMs in the District or Virginia. Here's some information about savings and checking accounts, credit cards, and local taxes.

Banking

One of your first decisions upon arriving in the Washington area is where to do your banking. A number of local banks have been acquired in the last few years by regional and national banks, so your previous bank might just have a branch down the road. For example, First Union of North Carolina has recently become a strong presence in the Washington area by acquiring the Dominion Bank.

Before opening savings and checking accounts at the bank closest to your home, remember that you won't always want to do your banking close to home. Some Washingtonians prefer to have a checking or savings account near the workplace to deposit a paycheck or use automatic teller machines. This is especially important if you live in one jurisdiction and work in another.

Also consider the banks' services and rules. With the arrival of deregulation, banks are free to charge for routine services and compute interest in a variety of ways. Interest rates vary greatly from bank to bank, and some offer additional benefits like PC-internet banking or ATM use at any bank's machines without incurring service charges. And don't forget to ask about traveler's checks, bank credit cards, and cash advances.

The law requires that banks give you access to funds from out-of-state checks after five business days. Lately, Congress has talked about cutting this number to three days. This is important when you are transferring funds to establish your Washington accounts.

Newcomers should consider selecting one bank for both checking and savings to establish a relationship with a local financial institution.

This will be helpful when you want to finance a home or automobile purchase or a home equity loan.

Below is a list of the names and phone numbers of those banks with branches throughout the Washington metropolitan area:

Chevy Chase Bank, 301/598-7100
Citibank, 800/926-1067
Citizens Bank, 301/206-6000
Crestar Bank, 800/451-2435
First National Bank of Maryland, 800/441-8455
First Union Bank, 800/398-3862
Nations Bank, 800/222-7162
Riggs Bank, 301/887-6000

Checking Accounts

Although each bank has its own application to open an account, they all require two references. Usually you will be asked the name of your employer and current or previous banking institution. You'll also need two signed pieces of identification: driver's license, passport, credit card, student identification.

Some banks require a minimum deposit to start a checking account, while others require a minimum deposit in order to receive interest. There are still other combinations of services, minimum balances, and service charges, so make sure you understand all the alternatives and choose the type of checking account that best suits your banking needs.

Your account will be opened immediately, but you'll have to settle for "starter" checks for a couple weeks until your personal checks are printed. In the meantime, you might want to pay bills and cut checks online, using software provided free by most banks to their checking customers.

Savings Accounts

Follow the preceding checking account guidelines to also apply for a "statement" savings account that provides monthly statements of all transactions and can be linked to your checking account. Of course, you can get just a savings account without opening a checking account at the same institution. Though not the case with all banks, most will require an average minimum balance. If you fail to meet this requirement, you'll have to pay a service charge.

Once you establish good banking and credit relationships, you can apply for a mortgage, loan, or bank credit card. ATM cards are issued automatically to new customers - but don't assume that ATM use is free. A recent and even more convenient card being offered by banks is a debit card. In lieu of writing out a check for a purchase, this card will withdraw money from your checking account. Generally, it's accepted anywhere major credit cards are accepted.

Credit Cards

Below are the major credit cards available.

- **American Express**, 800/528-4800. A Green Card costs $55 per year and requires proof of an income of $15,000 or over. A Gold Card costs $75 per year and requires proof of an income of $20,000 or over. Whereas Green Card holders cannot maintain a balance from one month to the next, the Gold Card entitles cardholders to a line of credit. The Platinum Card costs $300 a year, and American Express will notify you if and when you qualify for one. You'll be invited to receive a Platinum card after establishing a strong credit rating and charging over $10,000 a year on your Green or Gold card. The American Express Optima Card - regular, Gold and Platinum - offer standard AMEX benefits and a line of credit. American Express has branch offices throughout the District, Maryland, and Virginia. See your White Pages for a complete listing. If your card is lost or stolen, call Cardmember Services at 800/528-4800.

- **Discover Card**, 800/347-2683. The Discover Card is offered by Dean Witter Financial through Sears stores for no annual fee. The minimum income of applicants is judged on a case-by-case basis. Discover's Private Issue Card costs $40. Both cards offer users cash back at the end of the year. The basic card refunds up to one percent of your total purchases after $3,000 of use, and the Private Issue Card refunds 1.5 percent after the first $3,000 of use. If your card is lost or stolen, call Customer Service at 800/347-2683.

- **VISA** and **MasterCard**, can be obtained from various sources, usually banks, but even telephone companies, automobile manufacturers, and college alumni associations issue cards nowadays. Each card issuer has its own set of membership requirements, and some are completely eliminating the annual fee, or waiving it for the first year. Since it is possible to get a card without an annual fee, shop around — just be sure that the fee isn't dropped in exchange for a higher interest rate. There is little difference between VISA and MasterCard. Both offer similar services, and both offer Gold versions of the cards with additional services. Banks and department stores can legally charge up to 25 percent interest on credit card balances. But economic downturn and fierce competition have caused the rates to drop well below this rate of interest.

Department Stores will accept local personal checks for the amount of purchase, but with restrictions: two forms of identification — usually a drivers' license and a major credit card or department store card. In addition, some stores only accept checks printed with a customer's name, address, and phone number. Checks from outside the Washington area and third-party checks may be refused altogether.

Although virtually all of the major Washington area department stores accept American Express and/or VISA and MasterCard, many, including Bloomingdales, JC Penny, Hecht's, Lord & Taylor, Nordstrom, Sears and Uptons, issue their own credit cards. In fact, even stores like Ann Taylor, The Limited, and Express offer cards of their own.

Store charge cards offer advantages over the major credit cards: advance notice of sales, mail or phone orders, no annual fees, and in some cases, spreading payments over a period of time for an added finance charge. Store card applications ask for personal information like address and birthdate, bank and credit information, and employment information. In some cases the accounts are approved immediately, while others take a few weeks to verify information and approve your card.

Income Taxes

Federal income tax forms may be obtained from the **Internal Revenue Service** building at 1111 Constitution Avenue NW or at local post offices and libraries. Residents of the entire Washington metropolitan area can also get tax forms sent in the mail by calling 800/TAX-FORM, by ordering them through a fax retrieval system at 703/487-4160, or by downloading them from the IRS internet site at www.irs.ustreas.gov. For answers to specific federal tax questions, residents can call the IRS at 800/424-1040. The IRS offices are open 8:30am to 5pm, and while they will provide assistance, they won't do your taxes for you. If you want someone to do your taxes for you, ask a friend for the name of a good accountant, or look one up in the Yellow Pages.

State and local tax rates vary widely between the District, Virginia and Maryland. According to a recent Government of the District of Columbia study, "the District's overall tax burden ranks first at the $25,000 income level; third at the $50,000 [level]; second at the $75,000 level; and first at the $100,000 income levels." For more information on the comparative tax burdens across the three jurisdictions as well as specifics on the various taxes levied, contact the Office of Economic and Tax Policy at the Government of the District of Columbia's Department of Finance and Revenue and ask for a copy of their useful publication "A Comparison of Tax Rates and Burdens in the Washington Metropolitan Area." Their address is 441 4th Street, Suite 400; their phone number is 202-727-6027.

When you start your job, your employer will ask you which jurisdiction you reside in so that the appropriate state or local taxes are automatically withheld from your paycheck. For example, if you work in the District but live in Maryland, your employer will deduct Maryland state income taxes. The District of Columbia would like to tax the hordes of suburbanites who work in the city, but suburban representatives in Congress — which still has control over the District — have successfully squashed any discussion of a "commuter tax."

Maryland state income tax forms can be obtained at public libraries in Maryland and through the state **Treasurer's Income Tax Division**. Call 301/949-6030 for forms or information.

Virginia state income tax forms can be obtained at public libraries in Virginia and through the state's Taxation Department. For forms and information, call the **Taxation Department's Alexandria Field Office** at 703/838-4570 or Arlington Field Office at 703/358-3055.

District of Columbia city income tax forms can be obtained at public libraries in the District and through the city's **Department of Finance & Revenue**. Call 202/727-6170 for forms and 202/727-6104 for information.

Local city and town taxes are collected in some of the Maryland and Virginia suburbs. When you get state tax information, also inquire if your neighborhood is subject to local taxes as well.

Now that you've got a place to call home, and you've taken care of the basics like getting electricity and gas, you might benefit from some of the area's helpful services. Some of these services, such as furniture rentals, will help fill up an empty house or apartment. Others, including food delivery and house cleaning services, can make your life far simpler. Below are a few of the basics.

Carpool Services

Prince George's Ridefinders, 800/486-RIDE
Ride Finders of Alexandria, 703/838-3800
Commuter Connection of Arlington, 703/528-7969
Ride Finders of DC, 202/783-POOL

Consumer Services

Center for the Study of Services (publisher of *Washington Consumers' Checkbook*), 202/347-7283

Diaper Services

Dy-Dee Diaper Service & Cotton Bottoms, 800/492-9895
Modern Diaper Service, 301/853-3993

Dry Cleaning Delivery

Bergmann's Cleaning, serving DC, MD, and VA, 703/524-6764
Sterling Cleaners, serving DC and MD, 301/495-4912

Food delivery

A La Carte Express, serving DC only, 202/232-8646
Food Connection, serving Prince George's County only, 202/839-8898
Meals Express, serving Montgomery County only, 301/565-3030
Restaurants on the Run, Arlington County only, 703/527-9000

Takeout Taxi
> Alexandria, 703/719-9409
> Annapolis, 410/721-0002
> Arlington County, Capitol Hill, downtown, 703/578-3663
> Bowie, upper Prince George's County, 301/858-0002
> Fairfax County, Loudoun County, 703/435-3663
> Herndon, Reston, 703/435-3663
> Montgomery County, upper Northwest DC, 301/571-0111

Waiter on the Way, serving Montgomery County only, 301/869-0300

Washington's Green Grocers Organic Foods, 202/232-5556

Foreign Currency Exchange

Riggs National Bank, 1503 Pennsylvania Ave., NW, Washington DC, 301/835-6000.

Ruesch International, 700 11th Street NW, Washington, DC, 202/408-1200.

Thomas Cook Currency Services, 1800 K Street NW, Washington, DC, 800/287-7362.

Furniture Rental

Aaron Rents Furniture, 11714 Baltimore Avenue, Beltsville, MD 301/210-0120; 5720 General Washington Drive, Alexandria, VA, 703/941-7195.

Cort Furniture Rental, 11711 Parklawn Drive, Rockville, MD, 301/881-7388.

Furniture Rentals of America, 2784 S. Arlington Mill Drive, Arlington, VA, 703/671-8905.

Remco Furniture Rentals, 7069 Martin Luther King Highway, Landover, MD, 301/386-3333.

Scherr Furniture, 12340 Parklawn Drive, Rockville, MD, 301/881-8960.

House Cleaning

Cleaning Authority of Columbia, 410/290-3880
Cleaning Authority of Gaithersburg, 301/840-8353
Everclean Maid Service Inc., 703/971-7160
Maid Brigade, 301/949-4803

Lawn Care

Georgetown Lawn & Yard Maintenance, 202/333-1970
Green Thumb Lawn & Landscaping Service, 301/776-0212
Herman's Lawn & Gardening, 202/829-4595
Lawn Workers of America Inc., 301/816-7900
Shamrock Lawn Service, 703/742-6250

Mail/Receiving Services

Mail Boxes Etc., locations throughout DC, MD and VA, 202/686-2100

Metro Postal Inc., 785-F Rockville Pike, Rockville, MD, 301/762-3715

U.S. Postal Service, DC residents contact the customer call center, 202/635-5300. Maryland and Virginia residents contact your local postal station. (See Post Office listings in "Neighborhoods.")

Package Delivery

DHL Worldwide Express, 800/225-5345
Federal Express, 800/238-5355
Roadway Package Systems (RPS), 800/762-3725
United Parcel Service (UPS), 800/742-5877
U.S. Postal Service Express Mail, 800/222-1811

Pet Sitting

Alexandria Pet Sitting, 703/823-9225
Pets N Plants, 703/848-0700
Sit-A-Pet Inc.
    Arlington & Fairfax Counties, 703/243-3311
    District, 202/362-8900
    Montgomery County, 301/424-7100
Tender Loving Cat Care, 301/258-7745

Storage Spaces

Public Storage Rental Spaces, locations throughout MD, 800/44-STORE.
Storage USA, locations throughout MD and VA, 301/652-6565.

Services for People with Disabilities

Washington was ground zero for disability-rights activists from the late 1970s right up to the passage of the Americans with Disabilities Act. As a result, nearly every monument, museum, public transportation system, and office building is accessible to people with disabilities. The federal government and all major employers take affirmative steps to employ people with disabilities.

Gallaudet University, the only university in the country specifically designed for the deaf and hearing impaired, is in Washington, DC. Gallaudet is more than a college — it also has a model high school and serves as the center of deaf culture in the area.

That's the good news. The bad news is that many stores, restaurants, and theaters have yet to get the message on ADA. And strapped local governments have cut down on services for both adults and children with disabilities. (Check the government section of the phone book under Human Service Agencies, Disabilities.)

The District and every surrounding jurisdiction have specific offices for people with disabilities. There are also area-wide organizations serving disability groups.

- **Davis Memorial Goodwill Industries**, 2200 S. Dakota Avenue NE, 202/636-4225. A rehabilitation agency that provides training, placement and employment for people with disabilities.
- **D.C. Center for Independent Living**, 1400 Florida Avenue NE, 202/388-0033. The center helps newcomers and visitors locate emergency attendant care or a get a wheelchair repaired immediately.
- **Endependence Center of Northern Virginia**, 2111 Wilson Boulevard, Arlington, 703/525-3268. This center offers counseling and training for independent living for Virginians with disabilities.
- **Gallaudet University**, 800 Florida Avenue NE, 202/651-5000. A national university for the deaf and hearing impaired.
- **Lab School of Washington**, 4759 Reservoir Road NW, 202/965-6600. An innovative, ungraded school for children with learning disabilities. Also has night classes for adults.
- **Recording for the Blind — Washington Unit**, 4000 Albermarle Street NW, 202/244-8900. Provides books — including school texts — on tape.
- **Washington Ear — Metropolitan Reading Service For the Blind**, 35 University Boulevard East, Silver Spring, 301/681-6636. Provides recorded newspapers and other periodicals for the blind.
- **Washington Metropolitan Area Transit Authority (WMATA) TDD Information Line**, 202/6383780.

Washington, DC has one of the highest percentage of working mothers in the country, so child care is a major concern here. There are some companies and federal agencies, like the Department of Labor, that have on-site child care, but they are still in the minority. The number of parents seeking child care puts good programs at a premium.

Quality child care exists in the Nation's Capital — you just have to be able to pay for it and be prepared to do some research. There are three kinds of child care options: enrollment in a professional child care center, placement in a family child care home (both licensed and unlicensed), or hiring a baby sitter to come into your home. The price for any of these services diminishes as you go out from the center of the city.

Local governments provide lists of local child care centers, nursery schools, home day care providers and before- and after-school programs. Most lists are arranged by zip code.

- **Alexandria Department of Social Services**, 703/838-0750
- **Arlington County Child Care Office**, 703/358-5101
- **Arlington Public Schools Extended Day Program**, 703/358-6069
- **DC Department of Consumer and Regulatory Affairs**, 202/727-7226
- **Fairfax County Office for Children**, 703/324-7400
- **Montgomery County Child Care Connection**, 301/279-1773
- **Prince George's County Day Care Referral Network**, 301/864-4830

Child care providers are also listed in the Yellow Pages under "Child Care."

Nannies

There are a number of agencies which find nannies for a fee. Most will recruit for both live-in and live-out arrangements. These services tend to be pricey (they may charge up to $1,000 or the equivalent of the nanny's wages for four weeks.) but they often will refund your fee or replace the nanny if the arrangement doesn't work out.

- **A Choice Nanny**, 301/963-2229
- **All American Nanny**, 800/3-NANNYS
- **Childcrest**, 800/621-1985
- **Helping Hands**, 301/251-1475
- **Nanny Factor**, 301/320-5245; 703/764-9021
- **Nannies, Inc.**, 301/718-0100
- **White House Nannies**, 301/654-1242

Emergency Baby Sitting

Whether your sitter calls at the last minute to say she's sick, or you just haven't been here long enough to find a reliable teenager in the neighborhood, these companies offer last minute baby sitting services, but at a premium.

- **A Choice Nanny**, 301/963-2229
- **Chevy Chase Baby Sitters**, 301/916-2694
- **Mother's Aides**, 703/250-0700
- **Mothers-in-Deed**, 703/920-2454
- **Nanny Dimensions**, 703/691-0334

College Students For Hire

The going rate for college students is $7-8 an hour for summer nannies, part-time nannies, and occasional baby sitters. Here is a list of local colleges who will help you connect with a potential baby sitter:

- **American University** keeps a list of students interested in baby sitting. Send $1 and a self-addressed, stamped envelope to the AU Career Center, Attention: Job Corps List, 4400 Massachusetts Avenue, Northwest, DC 20016. If you have a permanent, part-time position to offer fax the information to 202/885-1861.
- **Catholic University** will post an ad for a month if you fax it to 202/319-4480.
- **George Mason University** accepts faxed information about your child care needs at 703/993-2361. You can also mail information to the Career Development Center, 4400 University Drive, Fairfax, Virginia 22030. The school newspaper will also take ads for baby sitters. Call 703/993-2942.
- **Georgetown University** will give you the names of students interested in occasional baby sitting. Call the campus employment office at 202/687-4187, or fax 202/687-6542.
- **Howard University** posts job descriptions if you fax the request to 202/806-2818.
- **Montgomery College** keeps a book of job openings. Fax information, including the age of your child, to 301/279-5089.
- **The University of Maryland** has a job referral service. To get your child care job listed, call 301/314-8324 or fax 301/314-9919.

Au Pairs

Women under age 25 (and a few men), usually from Europe, agree to provide a year of child care in exchange for airfare, room and board, and a small stipend. The au pair must have a private room and works a maximum of 45 hours a week.

These programs work better as cultural exchanges than as serious child care. As one Potomac dad told *The Washingtonian* magazine, "...If the au pair wants to go out and you need her to stay with the kids, what you have is a teenager who sulks in two languages."

The Congress has now written laws requiring the U.S. Information Agency to oversee and approve organizations arranging au pair services. The following eight meet USIA's standards. Only one is local, but all use local coordinators to match your family with the right au pair.

- **American Heritage Association/Au Pair International**, 800/654-2051
- **American Institute for Foreign Study/Au Pair in America**, 800/727-2437
- **Euraupair Intercultural Child Care Program**, 800/333-3804
- **Ayusa International/Au Pair Care**, 800/428-7247
- **Educational Foundation for Foreign Students/Au Pair EF**, 800/333-6056
- **World Learning/Au Pair Homestay**, 202/408-5380
- **InterExchange/Au Pair USA**, 800/287-2477
- **Exploring Cultural & Educational Learning/Au Pair Registry**, 800/574-8889

Other Leads

If you still haven't found the perfect child care solution, check out some of the following sources of information in your neck of the woods:

- Local parenting magazines, like *Washington Parent*, include information about baby sitters, child care, and nannies. There are several such free magazines, and they can be found in libraries and municipal centers.

- Churches and synagogues, large and small, often run their own child care programs or can recommend a good one. And don't feel that you have to be a member of the church or synagogue, or even of the same religion — more than a few young Christians are spending their days in Jewish day care centers.

- Bulletin boards throughout the area often list baby sitting services. Probably the best listings are in large supermarkets and in local universities' student unions. Just be sure to check references carefully.

As we mentioned in the introduction, Washington is a car town. The city's public transportation system was designed to be a substitute for cars, but the network of buses that were to have connected everyone to the subway never fully materialized. Those buses which do make it from subway to suburb often run only once or twice an hour. Even among those city residents who rely on the public transportation system to get them to and from work everyday, few can imagine life without owning or having access to an automobile.

Subway

Though not everyone can get to a **Metrorail** station easily, Washingtonians love their "Metro." It's safe at all hours, and stations are concrete cathedrals, where every trace of graffiti is removed within hours of it being spotted. Even the trains are clean and comfortable.

Many Metro-riders come from one-car households, and get dropped off at the nearest Metro station's "Kiss and Ride." Others park at one of the stations that offers parking for between $1.75 and $2.25 a day, and then ride the Metro to work rather than fighting traffic all the way downtown and then paying $8 to $10 for parking.

The subway runs through the District, Maryland, and Virginia, with five, color-coded lines criss-crossing the city. The system runs from 5:30am to midnight on weekdays, and 8am to midnight on weekends. Fares cost between $1.10 and $3.25, depending on the distance you travel and whether or not you're traveling during rush hours (weekdays 5:30am to 9:30am and 3pm to 8:00pm). You can get discounts for buying $10 or greater fare-cards. Several special Metro passes are also available, from day passes to two-week short-distance passes.

Metro passengers' biggest complaint used to be that the trains ran infrequently on weekends. Now there's "Metro Saturday Express," with trains running every ten minutes, free parking at Metro lots, and a $2.00 maximum for any one trip. Call **Metro** at 202/637-7000 for additional information. Fare-cards can also be purchased through TicketMaster, 202/432-SEAT, with only a small service charge.

Buses

- **Metrobuses** run throughout the District, Maryland, and Virginia. The lowest fare is $1.10, though it might be slightly higher depending on the distance traveled and whether or not it's rush hour. Since both Metro Buses and the subway are run by the **Washington Metropolitan Area Transit Authority (WMATA)**, bus riders can get transfer slips for reduced bus fares, or buy special subway/bus passes. Call Metro at 202/637-7000 for additional information.
- **Ride On** buses are run by the Montgomery County government to help connect people with the subway and Metrobus. Fares are $1.10 during rush hour and 90 cents during the mid-day and late at night. Two-week Ride About passes are also available. Call Ride On at 301/217-7433 for additional information.
- Alexandria's **DASH** connects people with neighboring **Fairfax Connector** buses, Metrobuses, and the subway. Most trips cost 85 cents, regardless of distance traveled. Special passes are available. Call 703/370-DASH for additional information.
- **Fairfax Connector** connects people with neighboring DASH buses, Metrobuses, and the subway. Most trips cost 50 cents, regardless of distance traveled. A Pentagon route, which only runs during rush hour, costs $1.35 to $2.05, depending on distance traveled. Special passes are available. Call 703/339-7200 for additional information.

Carpool Services

Carpooling allows you to save gas, do your bit to prevent air pollution, and in many cases take advantage of the area's faster and less congested HOV (high occupancy vehicle) lanes. If this sounds appealing to you, but nobody in your office lives just down the block from you, one of the following numbers might be able to put you in touch with other commuters who live and work near you.

Prince George's Ridefinders, 800/486-RIDE
Ride Finders of Alexandria, 703/838-3800
Ride Finders of Arlington, 703/528-7969
Ride Finders of DC, 202/783-POOL

Trains

- **Maryland Rail Commuter** or **MARC** train runs three lines between Maryland, the District, and West Virginia. The Camden Line runs from Union Station in the District to Baltimore Harbor and the Oriole's Camden Yards stadium. When the Orioles are playing at night, this line runs longer hours to accommodate baseball fans. The Brunswick line runs from Union Station to Martinsburg, West Virginia. The Penn Line runs from Union Station to Perryville, Maryland. One-way and round-trip tickets are available, and fares depend on distance traveled. Tickets can be purchased at MARC stations. Call 800/325-RAIL for information.

- The **Virginia Railway Express** is a new commuter train system that has a lot of potential but only a few passengers. One of its lines runs 40 miles west from Union Station in the District to Manassass. The other line runs 50 miles south from Union Station to Fredericksburg. Fares are based on distance traveled. Passengers can buy single-ride tickets, 10-trip tickets, or monthly, unlimited travel tickets. These tickets can be purchased at each Virginia Railway Express station or by phone. Call 703/658-6200 for tickets or additional information.

Taxis

Years ago the city taxi commission got rid of meters, divided the city into zones and subzones, and decided that all fares would be based on the number of zones between pick-up and drop-off. This system of zoning, with zone maps and fares prominently displayed in every DC cab, was intended to standardize fares and prevent taxi cab drivers from over-charging passengers. Unfortunately, the zone maps are difficult to under-stand and some drivers take advantage of unknowing passengers. For years there has been talk of returning to meters, and now the city seems determined to mandate their use, but continued protest by drivers con-cerned about the costs of equipping vehicles with meters will likely put their installation on hold.

You should also know that there are surcharges for rush hour travel, for each additional passenger beyond the first, and during snow emer-gencies. Cab drivers are also permitted to stop and pick-up additional passengers while you're in the vehicle. Also, drivers in Washington are often reluctant to use air conditioning in the summer, but upon request they are required by law to use air conditioning at the request of passen-gers from May 15 to October 15, and heat from October 16 to May 14.

Meters are used if you're traveling in Maryland and Virginia, or between one of these states and the District. District cabs that travel into Maryland or Virginia determine your fare based on the number of miles traveled.

You should have no problem hailing a taxi on a main thoroughfare in the District, so long as it's not raining. But good luck finding a cab in the suburbs! If you're not right near a Metro station, you'll want to call a cab. Here's a list of some taxi companies that serve the suburbs:

Barwood Taxi, 301/984-1900
Checker Cab of Montgomery County, 301/816-0066
Blue Top Cab Company of Arlington, 703/578-1111
Diamond Cab Company of Alexandria, 703/549-6200
Laurel Cab Company of Prince George's County, 301/776-0310

Car Rental

Several companies rent cars in the Washington area, including a number of local dealers, but here's a list of the national car rental companies and their phone numbers:

Alamo Rent A Car, National Airport, 703/684-0086
Avis Car Rental, 800/831-2847
Budget Car & Truck Rental, 800/527-0700
Enterprise Rent-A-Car, 800/325-8007
Hertz Rent A Car, 800/654-3131
National Car Rental, 800/328-4567
Thrifty Car Rental, 703/658-2200

Airports

Three large airports service the Washington area. Here's some information about them:

- **Baltimore Washington International Airport** is the farthest of the three from the city, but it's in a convenient location for Prince George's County and Annapolis residents. The airport's biggest draw now is Southwest Airlines, which offers low fares to Washingtonians willing to leave from BWI. For additional information about BWI, call 301/261-1000.

- **Dulles International Airport** is the beautiful, curved-glass structure featured in the movie "Die Hard 2." It's a large airport that's recently been doubled in size, and it has the longest runways in the area. No wonder you can get regular flights to Tokyo and Concord journeys across the Atlantic. Taking a cab from the District to Dulles is expensive; however, there are buses that run from various locations and subway stations to the airport. For additional information about Dulles, call 703/572-2700.

- **National Airport** is just a stone's throw from the District in Arlington. In light traffic, you can get from downtown DC to National in under 10 minutes. Or you can get there on Metro. National can't handle large aircraft because of its short runways, but it can finally handle its heavy traffic and crowds, thanks to the addition of new terminals and a taller tower. Shuttles to New York and Boston leave National every half-hour. For additional information about National, call 703/417-8000.

Until the 1980s, Washingtonians had limited shopping options. But then major national retailers and discounters took a look at Washington's demographics, and raced to get here. Today, there is an impressive range of stores to accommodate all tastes and price ranges.

Shopping malls abound in the Washington area, and locals have come to be mall-aholics. Washingtonians don't just like their malls, they love them, and visit them often. One-stop shopping is big, whether beds and bedding or cameras and VCRs are needed. As a result, you will not find this city has a plethora of great camera shops or carpet stores — these and other goods are found in the department stores or rugs-to-lamps furniture stores, which have beefed up their selections to meet local demand.

Vogue and *GQ* readers take note: Washington is a conservative fashion town. What shows up on the runways of Paris or New York could take years to get here — if ever. The length of skirts and the width of lapels remain fairly constant here. A Washingtonian walk on the wild side is a man in a pin-striped suit, a white oxford shirt, and a Mickey Mouse tie.

Washington stores are almost always open seven days a week. There are downtown malls: Chevy Chase Pavilion, Georgetown Park, the Shops at National Place, the Post Office Pavilion, and Union Station Mall. And there are suburban malls tied to the Beltway like Christmas lights.

One reason malls may be so popular here is that their extended hours fit the schedules of Washington workaholics and two-career couples. Mall stores open at ten in the morning and stay open until nine every night every day except Sunday. Sunday hours are generally noon until 6:00pm.

Full Service Department Stores

• Bloomingdales
In the late 1970s, the arrival of "Bloomies" was big news in Washington. Now overshadowed by both Macy's and Nordstrom, and beset by perennial financial problems, Bloomingdales has lost some of its panache. But its furniture collections are still unrivaled and its model

rooms are great for browsers looking for decorating ideas. Locations include Tysons Corner Mall, Dolley Madison Boulevard & Leesburg Pike, McLean, 703/556-4600; and White Flint Mall, 11301 Rockville Pike, Kensington, 301/984-4600.

• **Hecht's**
Owned by the May Company, a national retail giant, Hecht's has stores throughout the metropolitan area selling clothing, furniture, carpeting, curtains and drapes, appliances, toiletries, and linens. Hecht's carries moderate-priced merchandise rather than designer lines. Locations include 701 North Glebe Road, Arlington, 703/524-5100; Metro Center, 12th & G Streets NW, 202/628-6661; Montgomery Mall, 7135 Democracy Boulevard, Bethesda, 301/469-6800; and Tysons Corner Mall, Dolley Madison Boulevard & Leesburg Pike, McLean, 703/893-4900.

• **J.C. Penney**
Penney's had all but left Washington years ago, but returned in 1996 when Woodward & Lothrop, one of the city's oldest retailers, went under. J.C. Penney took over most "Woodies" locations, and immediately became one of the most prominent department stores in town. They sell everything from clothing to housewares to home furnishings - nationally known basics like Whirlpool and Levis as well as their own signature labels. Locations include Montgomery Mall, 7135 Democracy Boulevard, Bethesda, 301/365-5588; and Tysons Corner Mall, 1691 Chain Bridge Road, McLean, 703/448-9111.

• **Sears**
Several Sears stores have closed in recent years. The remaining ones continue to offer all the tools-to-toddler clothes and merchandise that Sears is known for nationwide. Locations include White Oak Center, 11255 New Hampshire Avenue, Silver Spring, 301/681-1700; Fair Oaks Mall, Route 66 & Lee Jackson Highway, Fairfax, 703/385-2299; and Montgomery Mall, 7103 Democracy Boulevard, Bethesda, 301/469-4000.

Other Department Stores

• **Lord & Taylor**
The "white glove" store still carries clothing and accessories for the traditional set. There are small departments for gifty home accessories and linens. Locations include 5255 Western Avenue NW, 202/362-9600; Fair Oaks Mall, Fairfax, 703/691-0100; and White Flint Mall, 11301 Rockville Pike, Kensington, 301/770-9000.

• **Macy's**
Macy's brought its New York attitude to Washington a decade ago. The stores' designer departments attract fashion-forward shoppers

of both sexes. Its "cellar" is on the top floor here — with great cookware and delicacies. Locations include Pentagon City, 1000 South Hayes Street, Arlington, 703/418-4488; and Tysons Galleria, 1651 International Drive, McLean, 703/556-0000.

- **Nordstrom**
  The arrival of this West-coast retailer just a decade ago shook up the Washington market. Nordstrom is known for quality and service. Its sales staff is actually helpful — a trait previously unknown in these parts. Nordstrom carries well-made clothing, cosmetics, toiletries, and accessories. It started as a shoe store and the shoe department carries such a wide range of styles and sizes that it is still unbeatable. Locations include Montgomery Mall, 7111 Democracy Boulevard, Bethesda, 301/365-4111; Pentagon City, 1000 South Hayes Street, Arlington, 703/415-1121; and Tysons Corner Mall, 1961 Chainbridge Road, McLean, 703/761-1121.

- **Saks Fifth Avenue**
  The Saks stores in Chevy Chase and Tysons Galleria carry top-of-the-line clothing and accessories for men, women, and children. A wide selection of formal evening dresses makes this a mecca for the charity-ball crowd. Locations include 5555 Wisconsin Avenue, Chevy Chase, 301/657-9000; and Tysons Galleria, 2051 International Drive, McLean, 703/761-0700.

Appliances

A smart way to buy appliances in the Washington area is to shop using the *Washington Consumers' Checkbook.* This not-for-profit publication rates local stores and services from health maintenance organizations to pest control companies. Several times a year, *Checkbook* issues "Bargains" with specific buys on appliances including televisions, stereos, refrigerators, etc. "Bargains" lists models and the prices specific retailers have agreed to sell them for. You may have to act fast — "Bargains" prices are available only for a limited period of time. *The Washington Post* Style Section lists a sampling of the "Bargains," but the full list is available only to subscribers. Checkbook also has a car buying service. To subscribe, call the Center for the Study of Services at 202/347-7283.

- **ApplianceLand**, 10801 Baltimore Avenue, Beltsville, 301/595-7360 and 866 Rockville Pike, Rockville, 301/762-5544.
- **Apache Appliances**, 28 Vital Way, Silver Spring, 301/595-7360.
- **Belmont TV,** 9101 Marshall Avenue, Laurel, 301/498-5600; 12500 Layhill Road, Wheaton, 301/498-5600; and 4723 King Street, Arlington, 703/671-8500.
- **Discount Electronics/Appliance Locators**, 2519 Ennalls Avenue, Wheaton, 301/929-0652.
- **Murrell's Electronics**, 2140 Wisconsin Avenue NW, 202/338-7730.

Beds & Bedding

- **Bed Bath & Beyond**, 12270 Rockville Pike, Rockville, 301/231-7637; and 5716 Columbia Pike, Falls Church, 703/578-3374.
- **Linens 'N Things**, has more than ten locations in the Washington area. Call 800/LNT-8765 for the store near you.

Futons

- **Atlantic Futon**, Idylwood Plaza, 7501 Leesburg Pike, Tysons Corner, 703/893-9125.
- **Custom Fit Foam and Futon**, 15809 Frederick Road, Rockville, 301/670-9090.
- **The Market**, 3229 M Street NW, 202/333-1234; 13048 Fair Lakes Center, Fairfax, 703/222-1200.
- **Mattress Warehouse**, has more than 10 locations in the Washington area. Call 301/230-BEDS for the store near you.
- **Urban Accents**, 3111 Duke Street, Alexandria, 703/370-1211.

Mattresses

- **Dial-A-Mattress**, 9385 Washington Boulevard, Laurel, 800/MATTRES.
- **Mattress Discounters** has more than 30 locations in the Washington area. Check your phone book or Yellow Pages for the stores near you.
- **Mattress Warehouse**, has more than 10 locations in the Washington area. Call 301/230-BEDS for the store near you.

Book Stores

Washington may have the most-educated residents of any city in the country, and the town is ruled by the printed word. So it is not surprising that there are hundreds of bookstores in the area. Whether you are looking for Tom Clancy's latest, or the last word on Shakespeare, you can find a bookseller who stocks it or will order it for you.

The national chains like **B. Dalton Booksellers** and **WaldenBooks**, have locations throughout the Washington area, mostly in shopping malls. **Borders Books & Music** has five area locations: 11301 Rockville Pike, Rockville, 301/816-1067; 5871 Crossroads Center Way, Bailey's Cross Roads, 703/998-0404; 1201 S. Hayes Street, Arlington, 703/418-0166 , 11054 Lee Highway, Fairfax, 703/359-8420; and 1800 L Street NW, 202/466-4999. Borders is known for its enormous selection and welcoming atmosphere. The stores offer comfortable reading chairs, classical music, and sales associates eager to assist you. The locations also have coffee bars. Giving Borders a run for its money, **Barnes & Noble** came to town in 1996, opening in the heart of Georgetown at 30th & M Streets NW, as well as in Bethesda, Falls Church, and Reston. **Crown**

Books, known for discounting bestsellers, started here and has now expanded its operations with **Super Crown**, introducing many niceties originally introduced by Borders. **Olsson's Books & Records,** which falls between Borders and Crown, also has several area locations.

There are also a number of booksellers catering to special interests. Among the good ones:

- **Book Gallery**, 4508 Walsh Street, Bethesda, MD, 301/654-8664. Owned and operated by The Writer's Center, this shop specializes in local poetry and small-press titles.
- **Cover to Cover**, Owen Brown Village Center, 7290 Cradle Rock Way, Columbia, MD, 410/381-9200. This bookseller specializes in New Age literature and books pertaining to women's issues.
- **Kramerbooks**, 1517 Connecticut Avenue NW, 202/387-1400. This small bookshop offers an eclectic collection, but its main draw is the fact that it opens early and closes late. The shop, as well as its attached cafe, Afterwords, are open all night on Fridays and Saturdays.
- **Lambda Rising**, 1625 Connecticut Avenue NW, 202/462-6969. This Dupont Circle bookstore carries gay and lesbian fiction and non-fiction titles.
- **Politics & Prose**, 5015 Connecticut Avenue NW, 202/364-1919. This shop is known for its strong selection on politics and its frequent readings by local authors.
- **Vertigo Books**, 1337 Connecticut Avenue NW, 202/429-9272. Vertigo has a wide selection of works related to international politics, world history and African-American studies.

Computers

There are now zillions of computer stores in the DC area - mostly in the suburbs. Computer prices change almost weekly, so the best way to get a good deal is to shop the ads in the newspapers. If you really know your stuff, be sure to check the business section of Monday's *Washington Post*, which includes pages of ads for local computer assemblers. These small companies often offer lower prices than the large chains, but their goods are not such name brands as Compaq and Toshiba. For consistent discount prices on name-brand hardware, check out these three chains:

- **Best Buy**, 1200 Rockville Pike, Rockville, MD, 301/984-1479; Pentagon City Mall, 703/414-7090, 6350 Seven Corners Center, Falls Church, VA, 703/538-1190.
- **Comp USA**, has locations in the Maryland and Virginia Suburbs. For a location near you, call 800/COMP-USA.
- **MicroCenter**, Pan American Shopping Center, 3089 Nutley Street, Fairfax, 703/204-8400.

If you want to rent a computer, call one of these stores:

- **American Computer Rental**, 11921 Rockville Pike, Rockville, MD, 301/762-8700.
- **Rent-a-PC Inc.**, 666 11th Street NW, 202/347-1582.

Furniture

- **Crate & Barrel**
  This national chain has opened a superstore with furniture on Massachusetts Avenue, just inside the District by the American University. It offers beautiful high-end modern and country traditional designs. 4820 Massachusetts Avenue NW, 202/364-6500.

- **IKEA**
  This Swedish home store specializes in sturdy wood furniture you assemble yourself and colorful home accessories. You can find real value here, if you don't mind hauling and building. The prices are reasonable and the selection is impressive. IKEA also offers custom upholstery and home delivery. Two amenities not to be missed: a kids playroom and a Swedish cafe with Scandinavian delicacies. IKEAs are located in the Potomac Mills Outlet Mall in Dale City, VA (703/494-4532) and at White Marsh Mall outside of Baltimore (410/931-5400).

- **The Hub, Levitz, and Marlo**
  Located throughout the Washington area, these stores are known for reasonable prices, wide selection, and few amenities. Don't expect high-end quality or designer styles here; but if you are looking to furnish quickly, these stores are good sources. Check the phone book for a location near you.

- **Pottery Barn**
  Originally a shop for home accessories and knick knacks, the Pottery Barn now sells the same type of country traditional furnishing as Crate & Barrel. (Not available in all locations.) 5335 Wisconsin Avenue NW, 202/244-9330; Tysons Galleria, McLean, 703/821-8504.

- **SCAN**
  Also located throughout the Washington area, SCAN features Scandinavian furniture in teak, rosewood, and walnut. SCAN also sells upholstered pieces, rugs, and home accessories. Check the phone book for a location near you.

- **Storehouse**
  Packed with storage systems and dining room furniture, you'll want to visit one of the chain's four area locations before you start unpacking boxes. Beds and couches are pricey here. Congressional

Plaza, 1601 Rockville Pike, Rockville, 301/231-7310; 6700 Wisconsin Avenue, Bethesda, 301/654-6829; 7505-J Leesburg Pike, Falls Church, 703/821-5027; and 809 S. Washington Street, Alexandria, 703/548-6934.

Hardware, Paints, and Wallpaper

Hardware superstores can be found in just about every neighborhood, whether you live in the heart of the city or the most distant boondocks. **Hechinger's** used to dominate the Washington market but **Home Depot** has made this a competitive corner of the retail market. Pricing battles are now common and service for do-it-yourselfers is stressed in both chains. Both also emphasize their ample selections. You should have no problem finding whatever you're looking for, whether it's an azalea, paint, a cordless weed-wacker, or roofing shingles. Check the phone book for store locations near you, or look under "Hardware" in the Yellow Pages. There are a few old-fashioned, neighborhood hardware stores where lights are dim and nails outnumber decorator accessories. A favorite is **Strosnider's**, located at 6930 Arlington Road, Bethesda, 301/654-5688 and 10110 River Road, Potomac, 301/299-6333.

Housewares

If the department stores don't have just what you're looking for, check out one of the following stores:
- **Builders Model Home Furniture Store**, 4500 Daley Drive, Suite 100, Chantilly, 703/803-1090 sells the contents of model homes including linens, silk greenery, and china.
- **Container Store**, 8508 Leesburg Pike, Vienna, 703/883-2122; and Congressional Plaza, 1601 Rockville Pike, Rockville, 301/770-4800.
- **Crate & Barrel**, Montgomery Mall, 7111 Democracy Boulevard, Bethesda, 301/365-2600; 4820 Massachusetts Avenue NW, 202/364-6100; and Pentagon City Mall, Arlington, 703/418-1010.
- **Hecht's Clearance Center**, 6200 Little River Turnpike, Alexandria, 703/354-9542 has some furniture, but is especially good for those looking for housewares.
- **Lechters**, discount housewares with locations throughout the Washington area.
- **Williams-Sonoma**, Mazza Gallerie, 5300 Wisconsin Avenue, NW, 202 244-4800 famous selection of professional cookery and hard to find utensils.

Garden Centers

Both Hechinger's and Home Depot dominate the garden equipment market in the Washington area and local nurseries often can't beat their prices on common shrubs and annuals. For more specialized service and selection, here are the top nurseries, according to *Washington Consumer Checkbook*:

- **American Home/White Oak Nursery,** 4641 Sudley Road, Catharpin, 703/754-2222.
- **American Plant Food,** 5258 River Road, Bethesda, 301/656-3311; 7405, River Road, Bethesda, 301/469-7690.
- **Behnke Nurseries,** 11300 Baltimore Avenue, Beltsville, 301/937-1100; 700 Watkins Park Drive, Largo, 301/249-2492.
- **Bennett's Nursery,** 1908 Beulah Road, Vienna, 703/938-6925.
- **Country Nursery,** 3330 Spencerville Road, Burtonsville, 301/421-9593.
- **DeBaggio Herbs,** 923 N. Ivy Street, Arlington, 703/243-2498.
- **Garden World of Virginia,** 11343 Lee Highway, Fairfax, 703/591-6619.
- **Homestead Gardens,** 743-W. Central Avenue, Davidsonville, 301/261-4550.
- **Merrifield Garden Center,** 12101 Lee Highway, Fairfax, 703/968-9600; 8132 Lee Highway, Merrifield, 703/560-6222.
- **Metzler's Nursery,** 10342 Owen Brown Road, Columbia, 410/997-8133.
- **Morning Glory Farm,** 2300 N. Pershing Drive, Arlington, 703/ 841-1576.
- **Roozen Garden Center,** 7610 Little River Turnpike, Annandale, 703/941-2900; 8009 Allentown Road, Fort Washington, 301/248-2500.
- **Stadler Nursery,** 6815 Olney-Laytonsville Road, Laytonsville, 301/840-2044.

Washington Area Antique Districts

Washingtonians love antiques — especially those residents of Georgetown and Northern Virginia who wish to fill their period homes with period pieces. So it is not surprising that you can buy everything but the ancestors themselves to achieve the to-the-manor-born decor. For pedigreed pieces, head to Georgetown's antique dealers, and be prepared to pay for the pedigrees. For more reasonable antiques, head out to Kensington, Maryland and Old Bowie, Maryland. You'll find Victorian oak furniture and stained glass dealers galore. For fifties funk and conversation pieces, Adams Morgan has a number of good stores.

Off Price Shopping

Clothing: Washington has a good representation of both in-town discounters and out-of-town outlet malls. For clothing, Washington shoppers flock to **Loehmanns** and **Syms** in the suburbs, **Filene's Basement** in the District, and the **T.J. Maxx** and **Marshalls** stores located throughout the Washington area. **Today's Man** in Rockville, Maryland and Bailey's Crossroads, Virginia consistently wins *The Washingtonian* magazine's consumer tests for both quality and price.

Outlet Shopping

There are three major outlet malls within easy driving distance of Washington:

- **Potomac Mills** in Dale City, VA is 40 minutes from the District on US 95 South. Anchored by IKEA and Wacamaw Pottery, Potomac Mills has clearinghouses for Saks Fifth Avenue, Macy's, and Nordstrom, and scores of manufacturers' outlets including Escada, Tommy Hilfiger, Georgetown Leather Design, and Calvin Klein. Potomac Mills has become the most popular tourist attraction in the state of Virginia.
- **Chesapeake Village Outlet Center** is at the junction of Routes 50 and 301 in Queenstown, Maryland just a few miles past the Chesapeake Bay Bridge. It is about an hour's drive from the city, and on the way to the beach for Washington vacationers. Anchored by Liz Claiborne, this upscale outlet complex has J. Crew, Geoffrey Beene, St. Johns, I.B. Diffusion, Bass shoes, and many other manufacturers.
- **Blue Ridge Outlet Center** is housed in the old factories of Martinsburg, West Virginia, just ninety minutes from Washington, DC. Ralph Lauren/Polo and Donna Karan have outlets here, along with Anne Klein, London Fog, Georgetown Leather Design, Country Road, Nautica, and dozens more.

Warehouse Shopping Clubs

These clubs have good prices on foodstuffs, cleaning products, paper products, office supplies, cigarettes, books, furniture, tires, eyeglasses, and an ever-changing array of seasonal and novelty items. However, you may have to buy in bulk, and there are no baggers, loaders, or delivery services.

Both Price Club-Costco Wholesale and Sam's Warehouses have locations in the Washington area. It used to be that club memberships were available only to self-employed individuals, federal workers, union members, credit-union members, and military personnel; but the competition grew fierce, and now anybody can shop in warehouses, although non-members pay a slight premium. Here's a list of locations:

- **Sam's Club**, 2365 North Highway 301, Waldorf, 301/870-7771; 8500 Landover Road, Landover, 301/386-5577; 610 North Frederick Avenue, Gaithersburg, 301/216-2550.
- **Price Club-Costco Wholesale**, 10925 Baltimore Avenue, Beltsville, 301/595-3400; 880 Russell Avenue, Gaithersburg, 301/417-1500, 4725 West Ox Road, Fairfax, 703/802-0372.

Other Sales

Every weekend, telephone poles along suburban thoroughfares are festooned with notices of yard sales. There are also ads in the local papers. Don't discount these sales. These are not junk sales — they can be sources for good furniture, appliances, linens, and housewares. Even affluent Washingtonians who are being transferred out of town or out of country routinely hold yard sales.

The Washington Post's Friday "Weekend" Section and *The Washington City Paper* have ads for flea markets, rummage sales, and church and school bazaars.

Washington is as diverse and vibrant a cultural, intellectual, and artistic community as you will find anywhere in the world —so many different people representing every U.S. state, every nation, and every interest have converged upon the Washington area, bringing their skills and styles, for over 200 years. From the stages of the Kennedy Center to the spectacular exhibits of the Smithsonian museums, Washington has more to offer than anybody would imagine from a city known almost exclusively for its politics.

If you want to find out the what, where and when of local events, here's a list of places to start:

- *The Washington City Paper,* which comes out on Thursday afternoons, provides the most detailed list of events for adults, from reggae concerts to poetry readings.
- *The Washingtonian,* publishes a monthly list of cultural events, hot performances, and movie reviews.
- *The Washington Post* and *The Washington Times* offer weekend sections publishing entertainment guides for the days to come. The *Post* version comes out in the Friday edition; the *Times* version comes out in the Thursday edition.

Tickets

TicketMaster sells tickets to just about every large area event, from concerts to sports. Call 202/432-SEAT or 800/551-SEAT to order tickets by phone. For smaller venues, call **Protix** at 703/218-6500. **Ticketplace**, located at George Washington University's Lisner Auditorium, sells same-day tickets to various local events at half-price. Call Ticketplace at 202/TICKETS for information.

Music

Classical—Professional

- **Library of Congress**, Coolidge Auditorium, 1st Street SE, 202/707-5502.
- **National Symphony Orchestra** at the John F. Kennedy Center for the Performing Arts, F Street & New Hampshire Avenue NW, 202/467-4600.
- **Wolf Trap**, 1624 Trap Road, Vienna, VA, 703/255-1868.

Classical—Community

- **Alexandria Symphony**, 703/845-8005
- **Arlington Symphony Orchestra**, 703/528-1817
- **Fairfax Symphony Orchestra**, 703/642-7200
- **Mid-Atlantic Chamber Orchestra**, 202/483-9320
- **Mount Vernon Orchestra**, 703/799-8229
- **National Chamber Orchestra**, 301/762-8580
- **New Columbia Swing Orchestra**, 703/524-4635
- **Washington Chamber Symphony**, 202/452-1321
- **Washington Civic Orchestra**, 202/857-0970

Opera—Professional

- **Washington Opera at the Kennedy Cente**r, Opera House, F Street & New Hampshire Avenue NW, 202/416-7800 or 800/87-OPERA.

Opera—Community

- **Maryland State Opera Company**, 301/384-4428
- **Opera Camerata of Washington**, 202/663-9018
- **Opera Theatre of Northern Virginia**, 703/528-1433

Ballet—Community

- **Washington Ballet**, 202/362-3606

Choruses—Community

- **Alexandria Choral Society**, 703/548-4734
- **Alexandria Harmonizers Barbershop Chorus**, 703/836-0969
- **Cathedral Choral Society**, 202/537-8980
- **Choral Arts Society of Washington**, 202/244-3669
- **Fairfax Choral Society**, 703/642-0862
- **Gay Men's Chorus**, 202/338-SING
- **Lesbian & Gay Chorus of Washington**, 202/546-1549
- **Mormon Choir of Washington**, 301/942-0103
- **Oratorio Society of Washington**, 202/342-6221
- **Paul Hill Chorale**, 202/364-4321
- **Thomas Circle Singers**, 202/546-7282

- **Washington Men's Camerata**, 202/265-8804
- **Washington Women's Chorus**, 202/244-5925

Jazz/Blues

- **Blues Alley**, 1073 Wisconsin Avenue NW, 202/337-4141.
- **Busara Club**, 2340 Wisconsin Avenue NW, 202/337-2340.
- **City Blues Cafe**, 2651 Connecticut Avenue NW, 202/232-2300.
- **New Vegas Lounge**, 1415 P Street NW, 202/483-3971.
- **One Step Down**, 2517 Pennsylvania Avenue NW, 202/331-8863.
- **State of the Union**, 1357 U Street NW, 202/588-8810.
- **Takoma Station Tavern**, 6914 4th Street NW, 202/829-1999

Live Alternative Music/R&B/Reggae/Rock

- **Bayou**, 3135 K Street NW, 202/333-2897.
- **Birchmere**, 3901 Mount Vernon Avenue, Alexandria, 703/549-5919.
- **Black Cat**, 1831 14th Street NW, 202/667-7960.
- **Capitol Ballroom**, Half and K Streets SE, 202/554-1500.
- **9:30 Club**, 815 V Street NW, 202/393-0930.

Large Concert Venues

- **Carter Barron Amphitheater**, 4850 Colorado Avenue NW, 202/426-6837.
- **Lisner Auditorium**, 21st and H Streets NW, 202/994-6800.
- **Merriweather Post Pavilion**, Columbia, MD, 301/982-1800.
- **Nissan Pavilion at Stone Ridge**, Manassass, VA, 800/455-8999.
- **Patriot Center**, 4400 University Drive, Fairfax, VA, 703/993-3000.
- **USAir Arena**, 1 North Harry S. Truman Drive, Landover, MD, 301/350-3400.
- **Wolf Trap and The Barns at Wolf Trap**, 1624 Trap Road, Vienna, VA, 703/255-1900.

Dance

- **Arlington Center for Dance**, 3808 Wilson Boulevard, Arlington, VA, 703/522-2414.
- **Creative Dance Center**, 3305 8th Street NE, 202/832-8535.
- **The Dance Place**, 3225 8th Street NE, 202/269-1600.

Clubs

- **Bank**, 915 F Street NW, 202/737-3177.
- **Cellar,** 2100 M Street NW, 202/457-8180.
- **Chief Ike's Mambo Room**, 1725 Columbia Road NW, 202/332-2211.
- **Club Asylum**, 2471 18th Street NW, 202/319-9353.
- **Crush**, 2323 18th Street NW, 202/319-1111.
- **Decades**, 919 E Street NW, 703/242-DOIT or 202/530-5261.
- **Madam's Organ**, 2003 18th Street NW, 202/667-5370.
- **Nick's**, 642 South Pickett Street, Alexandria, VA, 703/751-8900.

- **Planet Fred**, 1221 Connecticut Avenue NW, 202/331-3733.
- **Polly Esther's**, 605 12th Street NW, 202/737-1970.
- **Spy Club**, 805 15th Street NW, 202/289-1779.
- **Tracks**, 1111 1st Street SE, 202/488-3320.
- **Zei**, 1415 Zei Alley NW (off 14th Street), 202/842-2445.

Theaters—Professional

- **Arena Stage**, 6th & Maine Streets SW, 202/488-3300.
- **Ford's Theatre**, 511 10th Street NW, 202/638-2941.
- **GALA Hispanic Theater**, 1625 Park Road NW, 202/234-7174.
- **Kennedy Center, Eisenhower Theater, Opera House, Terrace Theater, Theater Lab**, F Street & New Hampshire Avenue NW, 202/467-4600.
- **National Theater**, 1321 Pennsylvania Avenue NW, 202/628-6161.
- **Olney Theatre Center**, 2001 Route 108, Olney, MD, 301/924-3400.
- **Round House Theatre**, 12210 Bushey Drive, Silver Spring, MD, 301/933-9530.
- **Shakespeare Theatre at the Lansburgh**, 450 7th Street NW, 202/393-2700.
- **Signature Theatre**, 3806 South Four Mile Run Drive, Arlington, 703/820-9771.
- **Source Theatre Company**, 1835 14th Street NW, 202/462-1073.
- **Stage Guild**, Carroll Hall, 924 G Street NW, 202/529-2084.
- **Studio Theatre**, 1333 P Street NW, 202/332-3300.
- **Warner Theatre**, 13th & E Streets NW, 202/783-4000.
- **Woolly Mammoth Theatre**, 1401 Church Street NW, 202/393-3939.

Theaters—Community

- **Actors' Theatre of Washington**, 202/667-5393
- **Chamber Theatre**, 301/657-2465
- **Church Street Theater**, 301/738-7073
- **Clark Street Playhouse**, 703/418-4808
- **Dominion Stage**, 703/683-0502
- **Encore Theatre Company of Washington DC**, 202/298-0811
- **Georgetown Theatre Company**, 703/578-4710
- **Horizons Theater**, 703/243-8550
- **INTERACT Theatre Company**, 703/848-2632
- **Metropolitan Theatrical Company**, 301/530-5211
- **MetroStage**, 703/548-9044
- **No Curtain Theatre**, 202/966-3670
- **Potomac Community Theatre**, 301/299-6803
- **Prince George's Publick Playhouse**, 301/277-1710
- **Reston Community Center Theatre**, 703/476-4500
- **SCENA Theatre**, 703/549-0002
- **Smallbeer Theatre Company**, 301/277-8117
- **Theater J**, 202/883-9665
- **Theatre Conspiracy**, 202/986-6184

- **Trumpet Vine Theatre Company**, 301/961-8537
- **Washington Shakespeare Company**, 703/418-4808

Dinner Theaters

- **Burn Brae**, U.S. 29 at Blackburn Road, Burtonsville, MD, 301/384-5800.
- **Keynote**, 5 Willowdale Drive, Frederick, MD, 800/722-7262.
- **Lazy Susan**, U.S. 1 at Furnace Road, Woodbridge, VA, 703/550-7384.
- **Show Biz**, 312 Main Street, Laurel, 800-SHOW-BIZ
- **Toby's**, South Entrance Road off Route 29, Columbia, MD, 301/596-6161.
- **West End**, 4615 Duke Street, Alexandria, VA, 703/370-2500.

Comedy Clubs

- **Comedy Connection**, 312 Main Street, Laurel, MD, 301/490-1993.
- **Headliners Comedy Club**,
  Holiday Inn, 2460 Eisenhower, Alexandria, VA;
  Holiday Inn, 8120 Wisconsin Avenue, Bethesda, MD, 703/379-HAHA.
- **Improv**, 1140 Connecticut Avenue NW, 202/296-7008.

Art Museums

- **Arts and Industries Building**, 900 Jefferson Drive SW, 202/357-4500, celebrates the centennial of America with items from the Victorian home and objects from the industrial revolution. Free admission.
- **Corcoran Gallery of Art**, 17th Street & New York Avenue NW, 202/638-3211, maintains a collection of European works from the 17th through 20th centuries and American works from the 18th through 20th centuries. Admission charged.
- **Dumbarton Oaks**, 1703 32nd Street NW, 202/338-8278, has a permanent collection of pre-Columbian, Byzantine, and classical works. Admission charged.
- **Freer Gallery of Art**, Jefferson Drive at 12th Street SW, 202/357-2700, showcases Asian, near-Eastern, and American works. Free admission.
- **Hillwood Museum**, 4155 Linnean Avenue NW, 202/686-5807, holds French and Russian decorative arts from the 18th and 19th centuries. Guided tours by reservation. Admission charged.
- **Hirschhorn Museum & Sculpture Garden**, 8th Street & Independence Avenue SW, 202/357-2700, for those who love modern art, this museum has 19th and 20th century paintings, sculptures, and an outdoor sculpture garden. Free admission.
- **National Gallery of Art**, East Wing, 4th Street & Constitution Avenue NW, 202/737-4215, houses a collection of 20th century art and often features spectacular temporary exhibits. Free admission.
- **National Gallery of Art**, West Wing, 6th Street & Constitution Avenue NW, 202/737-4215, holds a collection of both European and

American art works from the 13th through 19th centuries. Free admission.

- **National Museum of African Art**, 950 Independence Avenue SW, 202/357-2700, features such permanent exhibits as "Images of Power and Identity," "The Art of the Personal Object," and "Royal Benin Art." Free admission.
- **National Museum of American Art**, 8th & G Streets NW, 202/357-2700, is America's oldest art collection, containing works from the 18th century to the present. Free admission.
- **National Museum of Women in Arts**, 1250 New York Avenue NW, 202/783-5000, showcases paintings, prints, sculptures, and pottery by female artists. Admission is free but donations are requested.
- **National Portrait Gallery**, 8th & F Streets NW, 202/357-2700, holds portraits and sculptures of Americans, from common men to presidents to famous writers. Free admission.
- **Phillips Collection**, 1600 21st Street NW, 202/387-2151, is a modern-art museum known for its French Impressionist, Post-Impressionist, and American modernist works. Admission charged.
- **Renwick Gallery**, 17th Street & Pennsylvania Avenue NW, 202/357-2700, maintains a permanent collection of American crafts, paintings, and porcelains. Free admission.
- **Arthur M. Sackler Gallery**, 1050 Independence Avenue SW, 202/357-2700, displays Asian art including Chinese bronzes and Persian pieces. Free admission.

Museums

- **Anacostia Museum**, 1901 Fort Place SE, 202/287-3369, is a community-based museum of black history and culture, with an emphasis on the experiences of those in Washington and the upper South. Admission charged.
- **National Air & Space Museum**, 6th Street & Independence Avenue SW, 202/357-2700, maintains a collection of planes, rockets, and artifacts used since the first attempted flights. A favorite among children, the huge IMAX theater is not to be missed. Free admission to the museum; admission charged for movies.
- **National Museum of American History**, 14th Street & Constitution Avenue NW, 202/357-2700, is like many museums in one, holding everything from gems and coins to displays about Japanese-Americans and supercomputers. Free admission.
- **National Museum of Natural History**, 10th Street & Constitution Avenue NW, 202/357-2700, is another popular one with kids, with fossils, dinosaur bones, foreign cultures, and an insect zoo. Free admission.
- **Newseum**, 1101 Wilson Boulevard, Arlington, 888/639-7386, is a new attraction aimed at exhibiting news and news gathering, past and present. The museum, which opened in the spring of 1997, is completely interactive. Free admission.

• **U.S. Holocaust Memorial Museum**, 100 Raoul Wallenberg Place SW (just off 14th Street & Independence Avenue), 202/488-0400, opened in 1993, presents short films, exhibits, photographs, and artifacts from the Holocaust. Some parts may not be suitable for children. Free admission, but tickets are required. A limited number of same-day tickets are available at the museum. Advance tickets are available from TicketMaster (202/432-SEAT) and Hecht's department stores for a small service charge.

Movie Theaters

The multi-screen movie complexes are located throughout the city and suburbs. For a change of pace, check out one of the many films shown at the Smithsonian Institution. Also, embassies and cultural centers frequently present free films showcasing foreign lifestyles and film makers. Below is a list of those movie theaters which regularly show films or offer services not found at the general multi-screen complexes:

• **American Film Institute**, The Kennedy Center, F Street & New Hampshire Avenue NW, 202/785-4600.
• **Arlington Cinema 'N' Drafthouse**, 2903 Columbia Pike, Arlington, VA, 703/486-2345.
• **Bethesda Theatre Cafe**, 7719 Wisconsin Avenue, Bethesda, MD, 301/656-3337.
• **Cineplex Odeon Uptown Theater**, 3426 Connecticut Avenue NW, 202/333-FILM, #799.
• **IMF Visitors' Cente**r, 700 19th Street NW, 202/623-6869.
• **Key**, 1222 Wisconsin Avenue NW, 202/33-5100.
• **Library of Congress' Mary Pickford Theater**, 1st Street & Independence Avenue SE, 202/707-5677.
• **National Archives Theater**, 7th Street & Pennsylvania Avenue NW, 202/501-5000.

Clubs & Societies

Washingtonians are joiners. There are too many clubs and societies to list in this book. But if you're already a member of a national club, be it the Kiwanis or an Macintosh user group, check the phone book for a local listing. Also, local embassies maintain detailed lists of clubs that relate to their own country or culture, whether it's a Japanese flower arrangement club in Arlington or an Irish dance group downtown.

For more information on clubs and interest groups, check *Finding Fun and Friends in Washington* by Roberta Gottesman.

Culture for Kids

If your kids aren't happy in their new home, they'll make sure that you're not happy either. So it's especially important that your children feel like they belong here too.

Some of the museums listed above, like the National Air & Space Museum or the Museum of Natural History, are extremely popular with children because they offer hands-on exhibits or cover areas that fascinate youngsters. The National Zoo is another big favorite. And others, like the Holocaust Museum, have special exhibits for children. But there are also museums set up entirely for children.

Below is a partial list of activities for kids. Parents should refer to either *The Washington Post* or *Times* weekend sections for complete listing of local children's events and special exhibits.

Museums/Places to Visit

- **Capital Children's Museum**, 800 3rd Street NE, 202/543-8600, features exhibits designed exclusively for children, from ancient caves to modern animation. Admission charged.
- **Claude Moore Colonial Farm**, 6310 Georgetown Pike, McLean, VA, 703/442-7557, offers a view of a recreated 18th century family farm. Admission charged.
- **Discovery Creek Children's Museum**, 4954 MacArthur Boulevard NW, 202/364-3111, features living laboratories for environmental science, history, and art exploration. Admission charged.
- **Dolls' House and Toy Museum**, 5236 44th Street NW, 202/244-0024, displays antique dolls, doll houses, toys, and games. Admission charged.
- **Trolley Museum**, Northwest Branch Regional Park, Bonifant Road between Layhill Road & New Hampshire Avenue, Wheaton, MD, 301/384-6088, holds European and American trolley cars. Free admission, but charges for rides.

Sports

See "Sports for Kids" section of the Sports chapter.

Scouts

Almost every neighborhood has a troop or two. If you don't hear about it from neighbors, call the national offices listed here.
- **Boy Scouts of America**, 301/530-9360
- **Girl Scout Council of the Nation's Capital**, 202/337-4300

Theater

- **Adventure Theater**, Glen Echo Park, 7300 MacArthur Boulevard, Bethesda, MD, 301/320-5331.
- **Children's Theater of Arlington**, 2700 S. Lang Street, Arlington, VA, 703/548-1154.
- **Discovery Theatre**, Smithsonian Museum of Arts and Industries, 900 Jefferson Drive SW, 202/357-1500.
- **Puppet Company Playhouse**, Glen Echo Park, 7300 MacArthur Boulevard, Bethesda, MD, 301/320-6668.

Other

- **Arlington Planetarium**, 1426 N. Quincy Street, Arlington, VA 703/358-6070. Admission charged.
- **Goddard Space Flight Center**, Visitor Center, Soil Conservation Road, Greenbelt, MD, 301/286-8981. Free admission.
- **Library of Congress**, 1st Street and Independence Avenue, 202/707-5000. Frequently hosts exhibits and performances. Be sure to visit the recently restored Jefferson Building for a glorious step back in time.
- **National Aquarium**, Department of Commerce Building, 14th Street & Constitution Avenue NW, 202/482-2825. Admission charged.
- **National Zoo**, 3001 Connecticut Avenue NW, 202/673-4800. Free admission.
- **H.B. Owens Science Center Planetarium**, 969 Greenbelt Road, Lanham, MD, 301/918-8750. Admission charged.
- **Reston Animal Park**, 1228 Hunter Mill Road, Vienna, VA, 703/759-3636. Admission charged.
- **Rock Creek Nature Center**, 5200 Glover Road NW, 202/426-6829. Free admission.

Higher Education

Concerts, plays, lecture series, courses and lots of other cultural and educational opportunities await you at many of the area colleges and universities. Listed below are some of the main campuses. Look in the yellow pages under "schools -universities and colleges" for schools close to your neighborhood. Call the general numbers or look on campus kiosks for information about upcoming events.

- **American University**, 4400 Massachusetts Avenue NW, 202/885-1000. A liberal arts university with approximately 10,000 mostly full-time students (about half graduate, half undergraduate). The public is welcome to attend school performances, concerts, etc.
- **Catholic University of America**, 620 Michigan Avenue NE, 202/319-5000. The only university in America to be established by U.S. bishops, this school is well known for its theology and philosophy courses. There is also the renowned School of Music. If visiting, be sure to step over to the largest Catholic church in the Western Hemisphere, the Basilica of the National Shrine of the Immaculate Conception.
- **First Class, Inc.**, 1726 20th St., Washington DC, 202/797-5102. Offers weekend and evening career seminars taught by professionals from a given field. A place for professional and personal enhancement.
- **Gallaudet University**, 800 Florida Avenue NE, 202/651-5000. The largest university in the U.S. for the deaf and hearing impaired, specializes in graduate and undergraduate liberal arts programs.

- **George Mason University**, 4400 University Drive, Fairfax, VA, 703/993-1000. This school of about 23,000 has an equal mix of graduate and undergraduate students. Call the Center for the Arts, 703/993-8877 for information on upcoming speakers and performances, or the Patriot Center Concert Hall, 703/993-3000 for concert information.
- **George Washington University**, 2121 I Street NW, 202/994-1000. For those interested in the political sciences this is a good place to look for guest speakers on such topics. GWU specializes in offering courses in politics, government, and business. Call 973-1175 for GWU's Center for Continuing Education.
- **Georgetown University**, 37th and O Streets NW, 202 687-0100. Founded by Jesuits in 1788, Georgetown is known world wide for its School of Foreign Service. This is certainly a good bet in terms of visiting speakers and special events.
- **Howard University**, 2400 6th St. NW, 202/806-6100. Chartered by Congress in 1867 to educate freed slaves, it eventually established a reputation as America's "Black Harvard." While today this reputation is not quite as strong as it used to be (something the university says it is working on) its commitment to the liberal arts, especially its Afro-American Studies program, remains strong.
- **Learning Annex**, 1634 I St. NW, 202/639-2000. Offers a wide variety of classes, from business to planning your wedding to ballroom dancing.
- **Montgomery County Community College**, with campuses in Rockville, 301/279-5000, Takoma Park, 301/650-1300 and Germantown, 301/353-7700, this is a great place for credit and non-credit courses and seminars in your area of interest.
- **Northern Virginia Community College**, 3001 N. Beauregard Street, Alexandria, VA, 703/845-6200. Offers Associate degrees and both credit and non-credit courses.
- **St. John's College**, 60 College Avenue, Annapolis, 410/263-2371. St. John's offers a unique type of education. There are no majors or academic departments, only the liberal arts track called the Great Books Program. It's a four year immersion in the western classics, studying how art, music, and thought, shaped western history.
- **University of Maryland**, College Park, 301/405-1000. Beginning in 1990, the school embarked on an ambitious plan to make the University one of the best in the country. Top majors include Computer Science, Electrical Engineering, and Government and Politics.
- **University of the District of Columbia**, 4200 Connecticut Avenue NW, 202/274-5000. Offers both academic and non-academic courses. Call 274-6675 for non-credit and vocational classes in its School of Continuing Education.

T hanks to Pierre L'Enfant, the architect who designed the nation's capital, and the citizens and legislators who preserved his vision, Washington is greener than most other major American cities. The center of the city itself is a vast national park dotted with monuments, statues, and marble memorials. Since no building can be taller than the Washington monument, trees flourish, even on downtown streets. Other American cities can boast skyscrapers and steel canyons. Washington has 1,500 cherry trees, unspoiled waterfront, and softball fields and polo grounds within shouting distance of the Lincoln Memorial.

There are wide, green swaths of parkland on both sides of the Potomac River. These, like many other green spaces in the area, are maintained by the National Park Service. As a result, they are manicured and reasonably safe. The **C&O Canal Towpath** runs 23 miles from Georgetown to Seneca, Maryland and is a favorite for bikers, joggers, and fishermen. (The canal was severely damaged by storms in 1995 and 1996 so tourist barges were temporarily beached, but the path is restored.) The District of Columbia, Northern Virginia, and suburban Maryland also maintain regional and neighborhood parks for recreation and nature contemplation.

West Potomac Park (202/376-6695) is the green backdrop for the national memorials to Thomas Jefferson and Franklin Delano Roosevelt. Across the way at the **National Mall** (call the Public Affairs Office 202/619-7222 for general information about the memorial parks) is the Abraham Lincoln memorial as well as the stirring memorials for the veterans of the Korean Conflict and Veterans of the Vietnam War. **East Potomac Park** (202/426-6765) has one of the most unusual pieces of statuary in a city filled with statues — a half-buried figure known as *The Awakening* at Hains Point.

Rock Creek Park (Visitor Information Center is at 5000 Glover Road NW, 202/282-1063) is the green heart of the city. Eighty-five percent of its 1,800 acres is natural woodland surrounding the creek itself. Congress created the park more than 100 years ago when the area was rapidly becoming the unofficial city dump. Now Rock Creek is home to tennis courts, exercise, jogging, and bike trails, playgrounds and picnic areas. Beginning on Saturdays at 7am and ending Sundays at 7pm, Beach Drive, between Broad Branch Road and Ross Drive, is closed to vehicles so that skaters and bicyclers can wheel to their heart's content. **The Nature Center** (202/426-6828) offers lectures and guided nature walks. **Rock Creek Horse Center** (202/362-0117) has rentals, riding lessons, and a therapeutic riding program for children with disabilities. Visitors to **Pierce Mill** (near Beach Drive and Tilden Streets Northwest, 202/426-6908) can see grain ground into flour the 19th century way. The Mill is open Wednesday through Sunday, 9am to 5pm.

The National Zoological Park (3000 Connecticut Avenue NW, 202/673-4800 or 202/673-4717) houses more than 5,000 animals. The 160 acres have both traditional zoo exhibits and natural "habitats" like the Amazon Rain Forest re-creation which opened just a few years ago. There are several endangered species here and a nursery of newborns that fills in May and June.

The National Arboretum (3501 New York Avenue NW, 202/245-2726) was established by an act of Congress in 1927 to do research on trees and shrubs and educate the public about plant life. Today its 444 acres are filled with all manner of greenery from herbs to azaleas. **The National Bonsai Collection** was a gift from Japan to mark the Bicentennial and is over 300 years old.

Kenilworth Aquatic Gardens (Kenilworth Avenue and Douglas Streets NE, 202/426-6905) were created in the early 1800s by a Civil War veteran who brought lilies from his native Maine and planted them in an old ice pond on his property. Today 12 acres on the East bank of the Anacostia River are loaded with lilies and lotus — including the Egyptian blossom that was a favorite of Cleopatra. This is the only national park devoted to floating gardens.

Dumbarton Oaks Gardens (1703 32nd Street NW; 202/339-6400) is one of Washington's great secret gardens. The house is well known, but the formal gardens criss-crossed with brick walkways have received little international attention. Be warned — the steep inclines and steps make this difficult for those with strollers or mobility problems. Dumbarton also charges admission: $2 for adults and $1 for seniors and children 12 and under.

Hillwood Gardens (4155 Linnean Avenue NW, 202/686-5807) was once the Marjorie Merriweather Post Estate. There is a formal French garden, a greenhouse with 5,000 orchids, and a Japanese garden with a waterfall, lanterns and a bridge. Children under 12 aren't permitted and admission is $2.

There are two **Great Falls** parks — one on the Maryland side of the falls and one on the Virginia side. This is the spot where the Potomac River drops 60 feet. Virginians say they have the best view of Mather Gorge and the falls. Marylanders boast that they have better climbing trails along the rocky ledges of the Piedmont Plateau that formed the gorge. The two-mile Billy Goat Trail up and down the rocks is a challenge for climbers of all ages and makes visitors feel light years from the city. In fact, the heart of Washington is only 15 miles away. For more information about hiking clubs turn to the "Sports" chapter.

Theodore Roosevelt Island can only be reached from the Virginia side of the Potomac River. There is an exit on the George Washington Parkway that leads to 88 acres of wilderness. There is a bronze statue of Roosevelt, and a few miles of nature trails. Birdwatchers love this park. So do mosquitos in the summer.

For information about Washington-area parks, contact:

- **Arlington County, Department of Parks, Recreation, and Community Resources,** 703/358-4747
- **City of Alexandria, Department of Recreation, Parks, and Cultural Activities,** 703/838-4343
- **City of Fairfax, Department of Recreation and Community Services,** 703/385-7858
- **District of Columbia, Department of Recreation and Parks,** 202/673-7660
- **Fairfax County Park Authority, 703/324-8700**
- **Howard County Department of Recreation and Parks,** 410/313-7275
- **Maryland National Capital Park and Planning Commission, Montgomery County Department of Parks,** 301/495-2525
- **Maryland National Capital Park and Planning Commission, Prince George's County Department of Parks,** 301/699-2407
- **National Park Service, National Capital Region,** 202/619-7222
- **Northern Virginia Regional Park Authority,** 703/352-5900

Professional Sports

For weekly specifics on leading amateur and professional sporting events, check *The Washington Post* or *The Washington Times* sports section.

Baseball

Washington hasn't had a baseball team on its soil since the Senators packed up and left town three decades ago. Nonetheless, Washington baseball fans have found a home team in the **Baltimore Orioles**, who play in the beautiful, old-style Oriole Stadium at Camden Yards. The season runs from late March to early October. For general information about Orioles games, call the Stadium office at 410/685-9800. For tickets, call **TicketMaster** at 202/432-SEAT or 410/481-SEAT.

Camden Yards' Baltimore location might appear too far to go for a game, but MARC trains out of Union Station run to and from the stadium (See transportation chapter for additional MARC information). The ride takes about 40 minutes.

Basketball

The professional basketball season begins soon after baseball ends, and runs through April. The playoffs sometimes run through mid-June, though Washington is only starting to enjoy playoff fever, thanks to the addition of several strong, young players. Basketball fans are hoping that a 1997 name change, from the **Bullets** to the **Wizards**, and a move from the suburban USAir Arena to the new **MCI Center** in downtown DC, will lead to decades of success on the hardwood. And even if the team doesn't shine, games will at least afford sports fans a view of such stars as Patrick Ewing and the Shaq. For team information, call 301/NBA-DUNK. For tickets, call TicketMaster at 202/432-SEAT or 410/481-SEAT.

Football

Washingtonians love their **Redskins**, so much that the city essentially shuts down during game-time and anyone who even tries to mow their lawn during the game can be arrested for disturbing the peace. Of course, don't expect to attend a "Skins" game anytime soon - unless you are willing to pay a premium for scalped tickets — the waiting list for tickets is more than 10 years.

The football season begins with August pre-season games, and the regular season runs September through December. The Redskins played at RFK stadium for years, but the deceased owner, notorious Jack Kent Cooke, built a new stadium near Landover in Prince George's County. The new stadium is located about 35 minutes outside the city. The ticket office number is still 202/546-2222, though you should only call if you want pre-season tickets or to be put on the long list of patient fans waiting for season tickets.

Hockey

The professional hockey season runs parallel to basketball's, from October until April. Most years the **Capitals**, commonly referred to as the Caps, play through May in the playoffs before losing to division rivals.

The Caps also moved from the USAir Arena to the downtown MCI Center with the start of the 1997 season. For tickets, call TicketMaster at 202/432-SEAT or 410/481-SEAT.

Soccer

Major League Soccer came into being in 1996, and the local team is already a huge hit. **The DC United** won the MLS championship in its first season. Many of the team members are locals, having graduated from the University of Virginia. Others hail from top teams in El Salvador and Guatemala, which is one reason that the area's Latino community pack the games at the Robert F. Kennedy Memorial Stadium.

The United's regular season runs from April through October, with occasional breaks so that players can also play for their national teams. For tickets, call TicketMaster at 202/432-SEAT or 410/481-SEAT. Indoor soccer fans might also want to check out a **Washington Warthogs** game at the USAir Arena in Landover, Prince George's County. For tickets, call TicketMaster.

Horse Racing

Call these tracks for directions and information.
- **Laurel Race Course**, Route 198 & Race Track Road, Laurel, MD, 301/725-0400.
- **Pimlico Race Course**, Hayward & Winner Avenues, Baltimore, MD, 410/ 542-9400.
- **Rosecroft Raceway**, 6336 Rosecroft Drive, Fort Washington, MD, 301/567-4000.

College Sports

The Washington area is home to a number of colleges and universities, which means we've got exciting NCAA action in addition to the professional ballgames. When it comes to college ball in this area, basketball and football are all that really matter.

Basketball

- The **Georgetown Hoyas** for years played their home games at the USAir Arena in Landover. With the completion of the MCI Center, they'll move their play downtown to within a few miles of the campus. For tickets, call 202/687-4692.
- **George Washington University's Colonials** play in Foggy Bottom at their Smith Center. For tickets, call 202/994-6650.
- **The Howard University Bison**, a team that is finally starting to show some strength, play home games at their Byrd Gymnasium. For tickets, call the Cramton Auditorium at 202/806-7198.
- The **University of Maryland Terrapins** play their home games at Cole Field House. For tickets call, 301/314-8587.

Football

- **The Howard University Bison** play home games in Greene Stadium. For tickets, call the Cramton Auditorium at 202/806-7198.
- The **University of Maryland Terrapins** play their home games in Byrd Stadium. For tickets call, 301/314-8587.
- **U.S. Naval Academy** games are played in Annapolis at the Navy-Marine Memorial Stadium. With each point scored by the men in blue, the canons roar and the Midshipmen do push-ups. For tickets, call 410/268-6060.

Participant Sports

Local recreation and parks departments maintain parks, trails, and lakes, as well as tennis courts, basketball courts, and other community athletics facilities. Here's a list of their sports information numbers:

- **Alexandria, Department of Recreation Parks & Cultural Activities**, 703/838-4345
- **Arlington County, Department of Parks Recreation & Community Resources**, 703/358-4710
- **District, Department of Recreation**, 202/673-7660
- **Montgomery County, Department of Recreation**, 301/217-6790
- **Prince George's County, Maryland-National Capital Park & Planning Commission**, 301/699-2400

Basketball

The courts are usually kept up by the recreation departments. Call one of the numbers listed above for court and league information. Below is a list of a few pick-up games that are always open to newcomers.

- **Drop-in Play**, Laurel Armory Community Center in Laurel, Sundays 11am-1pm, 301/497-0300.
- **Men's Pickup Games**, Ramsay Recreation Center in Alexandria, Mondays & Wednesdays 8-10pm, Saturdays 2-6pm, 703/838-4826.
- **Thirty & Over Open Play**, Charles Barrett Center in Alexandria, Tuesdays & Thursdays 8-10pm, 703/838-4818.
- **Women's 5-on-5**, Seat Pleasant Recreation Center, Wednesdays 6-8pm, 301/773-6685.

Bicycling

Whether you are in training for the Tour de France or just want to spend a day biking around the area, you will have no problem finding a nice place to ride. Around here, the hotspots are the **C&O Canal Towpath**, **Mount Vernon Trail**, and **Rock Creek Park**. Serious mountain bikers should be sure to not ride in areas where bicycles are prohibited, and parents should be advised that several jurisdictions require all persons under 18 to wear a bicycle helmet — bicyclists, or in the latter case their parents, can be issued warning citations or fined. Here are several bicycling clubs and touring groups for those interested:

- **Arlington Cycling Club**, 202/543-6546
- **Bike the Sites, Inc.**, 202/966-8662
- **Potomac Pedallers Touring Club**, 202/363-TOUR

The following shops offer bicycle rentals:

- **Big Wheel Bikes**, 1034 33rd Street NW, 202/337-0254; Two Prince Street, Alexandria, VA, 703/739-2300.
- **City Bikes**, 2501 Champlain Street NW, 202/265-1564.
- **Fletcher's Boat House**, 4940 Canal Road NW, 202/244-0461.
- **Metropolis Bike & Scooter, Inc.**, 709 8th St. SE, 202 543-8900.
- **Washington Sailing Marina**, George Washington Parkway, Alexandria, VA, 703/548-9027.

Boating/Sailing/Windsurfing

When you've got the itch to paddle, row, or fly with the wind, here's a list of stores and marinas which offer rentals of all kinds. On the Potomac, local boat owners can get a wet or dry slip at either Belle Haven or Washington Sailing Marina. Chesapeake Bay boaters, though, should be warned that there's a waiting list for just about every marina near Annapolis.

- **Belle Haven Marina**, Belle Haven Road & George Washington Parkway, Alexandria, VA, 703/768-0018.
- **Fletcher's Boat House**, 4940 Canal Road NW, 202/244-0461.
- **Thompson's Boat Center**, Rock Creek Parkway & Virginia Avenue NW, 202/333-4861.
- **Washington Sailing Marina**, George Washington Parkway, Alexandria, VA, 703/548-9027.

Curling

This recent addition to the Winter Olympics is gaining popularity worldwide. If you want to try it, and it's cold enough, call the **Potomac Curling Club** at 410/715-1655.

Fishing

There are a number of area rivers and lakes practically brimming with fish, and the ocean is just a few hours away. After one day on the Chesapeake Bay, you'll know how Maryland got its slogan, "Maryland is for Crabs." No doubt you can catch one "this" big, just be sure to obey local fishing laws. Since they vary from one jurisdiction to another, ask for details at your local bait and tackle shop, this is also the place to pick up your fishing license. Here are three area clubs for fishing enthusiasts:

- **Fishbusters Club**, 301/292-8377
- **Potomac Bassmasters**, 301/567-3030
- **Potomac River Smallmouth Club**, 703/444-2429

Frisbee

If you consider it "The Ultimate Sport," you might want to join like-minded people in the **Washington Area Frisbee Club**, 301/558-2629. For those newcomers who enjoy or want to try Disc Golf, you'll be pleased to learn that several public parks have created courses. You can get information about them by calling your local recreation and parks department, or by calling the **Washington Area Disc League** during the day at 703/765-2950 or in the evening at 703/280-5176.

Golf

The Washington area is packed with golf courses, both public and private. There are just too many public courses to list here, so check your Yellow Pages under "Golf" or call your local recreation and parks department for the location near you. To play on a private course, you'll either have to join one of the area's exclusive country clubs or go as the guest of a current member.

Hiking

There are numerous trails in and around the Washington area, especially if you are willing to drive west to **Shenandoah National Park** in the Blue

Ridge Mountains. If you want a simple hike without a long drive, try **Great Falls National Park**, or on the Maryland side of the Potomac, **Carderock**. The **Billy Goat Trail** is especially good for beginners. Turn to the "Green Space" chapter of this book for more information about area parks.

Also, a number of groups provide organized outdoor enjoyment for hikers and nature lovers.

- **Appalachian Mountain Club**, 202/298-1488
- **Northern Virginia Hiking Club**, 703/440-1805
- **Potomac Appalachian Trail Club**, 703/242-0965
- **Potomac Backpackers**, 703/524-1185
- **Sierra Club**, 202/547-2326
- **Washington Women Outdoors**, 301/864-3070

Horseback Riding

You won't see many horses trotting around downtown, and if you do they will most likely carry U.S. Park Police officers. But there are several places in and around town that will help city slickers become urban cowboys, and cowgirls. Here's a partial list:

- **Cavallo Farm**, a boarding, lesson and training farm, Highway 659, Chantilly, VA, 703/327-6431.
- **Meadowbrook Stables**, Meadowbrook Lane & East-West Highway, Chevy Chase, MD, 301/589-9026.
- **Rock Creek Park Horse Centre**, 5100 Glover Road NW, 202/362-0117.
- **Wheaton Park Stables**, 1101 Glenallen Avenue, Wheaton, MD, 301/622-3311.

Ice Skating

There are more than a few public rinks located throughout Washington's surrounding suburbs. In the District, there's one rink behind the White House on the Ellipse and another on the Mall between the National Gallery of Art and the Museum of Natural History. The Park Service also allows skaters to use the C&O Canal and Lincoln Monument's Reflecting Pool when the ice is more than three inches thick. Call the recreation and parks departments for locations near you. (See listings at end of chapter.)

In-line Skating

Park rangers will vigorously defend blacktop around national monuments from in-line skaters, but there are many other places to go, including the paths along the Potomac River and Rock Creek Park. Beginning on Saturdays at 7am and ending Sundays at 7pm, Beach Drive, between Broad Branch Road and Ross Drive, is closed to vehicles and open to skaters and bicyclers. The **Washington Area Rollerskaters** can provide information about local events and lessons. Call the group at 202/466-5005.

You can also rent in-line skates at **City Bikes**, 2501 Champlain Street NW, 202/265-1564 or the **Ski Center**, 49th Street & Massachusetts Avenue NW, 202/966-4474.

Polo

Most people in Washington stick to wearing Polo rather than playing it. But if you're one of the few and proud, or you just want to watch, call the **Potomac Polo Club**, at 301/972-7757. Also, during the spring and summer there are occasional Sunday polo matches on the Mall, near the Lincoln Memorial.

Rock Climbing

Close to home, climbers will find 20- to 50-foot rock faces along the Potomac River, at **Carderock** on the Maryland side of the river and **Great Falls** on the Virginia side. For those willing to drive about 200 miles, the **Spruce Knob-Seneca Rocks National Recreation Area** in West Virginia is the place to climb. This park offers experienced climbers huge arches and vertical rock towers. For indoor climbing or lessons, **Sport Rock** has locations in Maryland and Virginia. Call 703/212-ROCK for the location near you.

Running

The White House has its own running track, but it seems most people downtown - including the President - run on the Mall or along the banks of the Potomac River. Others love the shaded rolling hills of Rock Creek Park. Here's a list of groups that you might want to join:

- **American Running & Fitness Association**, 301/913-9517
- **DC Road Runners**, 703/241-0395
- **Reston Runners**, 703/437-3668
- **Washington Running Club**, 703/536-7764

Soccer Leagues

Soccer just keeps getting more and more popular in the area. The local adult leagues seem to keep changing, but the **U.S. Soccer Federation** (312/808-1300) or **Metropolitan DC/Virginia/Maryland Soccer Association** (703/321-7254) can provide you with the latest league information and put you in touch with leaders near you.

Swimming

It gets pretty hot and humid during a typical Washington summer, and a brief dip in the pool is always nice when you can't make it to the beach. There are plenty of pools in the area, both pubic and private. In Arlington County and the District, some public high schools are open to the public when not in use by the schools. Call your local high school for additional information. Or call the local recreation and parks departments for locations of swimming pools and aquatics centers near you. Below are the department telephone numbers:

- **Alexandria**, 703/838-4343
- **Arlington County**, 703/358-6262
- **District**, 202/576-6436
- **Fairfax County**, 703/246-5601
- **Montgomery County**, 301/217-6840
- **Prince George's County**, 301/249-7200

Tennis

There are courts scattered all over the Washington area. In addition to those at private clubs, there are courts in most parks and at just about every junior and senior high school. Still, on nice days every court in town will be occupied, and you might have to wait a while just to get in an hour of play before another group takes your spot. Montgomery County residents can call 301/217-6860 for information about outdoor courts. Residents of all other parts of the area should call your local recreation and parks department. (See listings at end of chapter.)

Health Clubs

Not everyone in town goes to a health club, but just about everybody here is a member of one.

The Washington area has an abundance of athletic facilities, ranging from no-frills free-weight rooms to centers with everything from indoor jogging tracks and tennis courts to Nautilus rooms and rows of Lifecycles. Many mid-level and upscale hotels have also opened their gyms to those willing to pay annual memberships - often for much less than other area clubs. Below are some of the places which offer a variety of exercise options:

- **Bally's Total Fitness Centers**, locations throughout the area, 800/695-8111.
- **Chevy Chase Athletic Club**, 5454 Wisconsin Avenue, Chevy Chase, MD, 301/656-8834.
- **Fitness Company at Georgetown**, 1010 Wisconsin Avenue NW, 202/625-9100.
- **Loew's Fitness & Swim**, L'Enfant Plaza SW, 202/646-4450.
- **Results**, 17th & U Streets NW, 202/518-0001.
- **Sport & Health**, locations throughout the area, 703/556-6550.
- **Sport Fit**, locations throughout the area, 202/887-0760.
- **Washington Sports Club**, locations throughout the area, 202/332-0100.
- **YMCA**, locations throughout the area, 202/232-6700.
- **YWCA Fitness Center at Gallery Place**, 624 9th Street NW, 202/626-0710.

Sports for Kids

Local recreation departments run a number of sports programs for kids, offering everything from basketball to softball. Call your local recreation department for information about particular sports and seasons. Probably the only sport not offered is soccer, so a large number of leagues have sprung up to fill the gap. The **U.S. Soccer Federation** (312/808-1300) or **Metropolitan DC/Virginia/Maryland Soccer Association** (703/321-7254) can put you in touch with a local league, or call the groups listed below:

- **Youth Soccer Leagues**
- **Alexandria Soccer Association, Inc.**, 703/684-5425
- **Annandale Boys Club Inc.**, 703/941-4410
- **Arlington Soccer**, 703/532-2088
- **Bethesda Soccer Club**, 301/871-2268
- **Fairfax Police Youth Club**, 703/591-3792
- **Gaithersburg Parks & Recreation Soccer**, 301/258-6350
- **National Capital Soccer League Inc.**, 703/385-1608
- **Springfield Youth Club**, 703/455-8554
- **Stoddert DC Club**, 202/965-4625

For information about Washington-area parks, contact:

- **Arlington County, Department of Parks, Recreation, and Community Resources**, 703/358-4747
- **City of Alexandria, Department of Recreation, Parks, and Cultural Activities**, 703/838-4343
- **City of Fairfax, Department of Recreation and Community Services**, 703/385-7858
- **District of Columbia, Department of Recreation and Parks**, 202/673-7660
- **Fairfax County Park Authority**, 703/324-8700
- **Howard County Department of Recreation and Parks**, 410/313-7275
- **Maryland National Capital Park and Planning Commission, Montgomery County Department of Parks**, 301/495-2525
- **Maryland National Capital Park and Planning Commission, Prince George's County Department of Parks**, 301/699-2407
- **National Park Service, National Capital Region**, 202/619-7222
- **Northern Virginia Regional Park Authority**, 703/352-5900

There is no predominant religion in the Washington area. There might be more Jews in the Maryland suburbs than in the Virginia suburbs, and more Muslims in DC than in the neighboring suburbs, but overall the people who converged upon the city over the years have brought their religions with them, and just about every denomination under the sun has a place of worship somewhere in the area.

Choosing a place of worship is a personal decision. The list in this guide is in no way complete, but rather a place to start until you have a feel for the Washington area. You might get the best advice from new neighbors, colleagues, or acquaintances. If you want a more complete list of places of worship, check the Yellow Pages under "Churches" and "Synagogues."

Churches

Baptist

- **Bethesda First Baptist Church**, 5033 Wilson Lane, Bethesda, MD, 301/654-4159.
- **Canaan Baptist Church**, 1607 Monroe Street NW, 202/234-5330.
- **First Baptist Church of Alexandria**, 2932 King Street, Alexandria, VA, 703/684-3720.
- **First Baptist Church of Chesterbrook**, 1740 Kirby Road, McLean, VA, 703/356-7088.
- **Iglesia Bautista Hispana De Gaithersburg**, 1004 Quince Orchard Road, Gaithersburg, MD, 301/216-1453.
- **Saint Stephen's Baptist Church**, 628 M Street NW, 202/289-1665.

Catholic

- **Basilica of the National Shrine of the Immaculate Conception**, Michigan Avenue & 4th Street NE, 202/526-8300.
- **Holy Martyrs of Vietnam Church**, 915 S. Wakefield Street, Arlington, VA, 703/553-0370.
- **Saint Bartholomew's Church**, 7212 Blacklock Road, Bethesda, MD, 301/229-7933.

- **Saint Dominic's Church**, 630 E Street SW, 202/554-7863.
- **Saint Thomas A. Becket Catholic Church**, 1421 Wiehle Avenue, Reston, VA, 703/437-7113.
- **Shrine of the Most Blessed Sacrament**, 6001 Western Avenue NW, 202/966-6575.

Episcopal

- **All Saints' Church**, 3 Chevy Chase Circle, Bethesda, MD, 301/654-2488.
- **Saint Francis Episcopal Church**, 9220 Georgetown Pike, Great Falls, VA, 703/759-2082.
- **Saint James Episcopal Church**, 11815 Seven Locks Road, Potomac, MD, 301/762-8040.
- **Saint John's Episcopal Church-Georgetown Parish**, 3240 O Street NW, 202/338-1796.
- **Truro Episcopal Church**, 10520 Main Street, Fairfax, VA, 703/273-1300.
- **Washington National Cathedral**, Wisconsin & Massachusetts Avenues NW, 202/537-6200.

Interdenominational

- **Church of Love Faith Center**, 4708 14th Street NW, 202/723-3411.
- **Mount Calvary Community Church**, 6731 Beulah Street, Alexandria, VA, 703/971-0165.
- **New Covenant Fellowship Church**, 1455 Research Boulevard, Rockville, MD, 301/309-0203.
- **Solid Rock Church**, 5401 Good Luck Road, Riverdale, MD, 301/474-7800.
- **Universal Meditation Temple of Deliverance**, 734 Longfellow Street NW, 202/723-7518.

Jehovah's Witnesses

- **Jehovah's Witnesses**, 624 Great Falls Road, Rockville, MD, 301/340-0217.
- **Jehovah's Witnesses Centreville Congregation**, 3701 Jermantown Road, Fairfax, VA, 703/691-3902.
- **Jehovah's Witnesses Kensington Congregation**, 11235 Newport Mill Road, Kensington, MD, 301/933-2119
- **Jehovah's Witnesses Kingdom Hall**, 6110 Princess Garden Parkway, Lanham, MD, 301/577-4488.
- **Jehovah's Witnesses Northern Virginia Congregation**, 6 E. Masonic View Avenue, Alexandria, VA, 703/836-6030.
- **Jehovah's Witnesses Spring Valley**, 2950 Arizona Avenue NW, 202/966-1705.

Lutheran

- **Advent Lutheran Church LCA**, 222 S. Arlington Ridge Road, Arlington, VA, 703/521-7010.
- **Bethany Lutheran Church**, 2501 Beacon Hill Road, Alexandria, VA, 703/765-8255.
- **Christ Lutheran Church of Bethesda**, 8011 Old Georgetown Road, Bethesda, MD, 301/652-5160.
- **Georgetown Lutheran Church**, 1556 Wisconsin Avenue NW, 202/337-9070.
- **Saint Paul's Lutheran Church**, 4900 36th Street NW, 202/966-5489.
- **Zion Evangelical Lutheran Church**, 7410 New Hampshire Avenue, Takoma Park, MD, 301/434-0444.

Methodist

- **Alberta Gary Memorial United Church**, 9405 Guilford Road, Columbia, MD, 301/498-7879.
- **Ashbury Methodist Church**, 11th & K Streets NW, 202/628-0009.
- **Congress Heights United Methodist Church**, 421 Alabama Avenue SE, 202/562-0600.
- **Great Falls United Methodist Church**, 10100 Georgetown Pike, Great Falls, VA, 703/759-3705.
- **Mount Olivet United Methodist Church**, 1500 N. Glebe Road, Arlington, VA, 703/527-3934.
- **Saint Paul's United Methodist Church**, 10401 Armory Avenue, Kensington, MD, 301/933-7933.
- **Wesley United Methodist Church**, 8412 Richmond Avenue, Alexandria, VA, 703/780-5019.

Non-denominational

- **Gospel Spreading Church**, 1522 R Street NW, 202/387-1471.
- **Grace Chapel of Washington**, DC, 4115 Muncaster Mill Road, Rockville, MD, 301/924-2515.
- **Harvest Christian Fellowship**, 1485 Chain Bridge Road, McLean, VA, 703/790-0102.
- **House of Prayer**, 3725 Ridgelea Drive, Fairfax, VA, 703/425-7437.
- **Victory Church**, 3149 Annandale Road, Falls Church, VA, 703/534-3337.
- **Washington Christian Assembly**, 30 Kennedy Street NW, 202/726-2100.

Orthodox

- **Greek Orthodox Church of Saint George**, 7701 Bradley Boulevard, Bethesda, MD, 301/469-7990.
- **Russian Orthodox Church of Saint Nicholas of the Orthodox Church of America**, 3500 Massachusetts Avenue NW, 202/333-5060.

- **Saint George's Antiochian Orthodox Christian Church**, 4335 16th Street NW, 202/723-5335 or 301/816-9541.

Presbyterian

- **Arlington Presbyterian Church**, 3507 Columbia Pike, Arlington, VA, 703/920-5660.
- **Chevy Chase Presbyterian Church**, 1 Chevy Chase Circle NW, 202/363-2202.
- **Fifteenth Street Presbyterian Church**, 1701 15th Street NW, 202/234-0300.
- **Heritage Presbyterian Church**, 8503 Fort Hunt Road, Alexandria, VA, 703/360-9546.
- **National Presbyterian Church**, 4101 Nebraska Avenue NW, 202/537-0800.
- **Potomac Presbyterian Church**, 10301 River Road, Potomac, MD, 301/299-6007.
- **Takoma Park Presbyterian Church**, 310 Tulip Avenue, Takoma Park, MD, 301/270-5550.

Seventh-Day Adventist

- **Capital Memorial Seventh-Day Adventist Church**, 3150 Chesapeake Street NW, 202/362-3668.
- **Capitol Hill Seventh-Day Adventist Church**, 914 Massachusetts Avenue SE, 202/543-1344.
- **Emmanuel Temple Seventh-Day Adventist Church**, 2707 DeWitt Avenue, Alexandria, VA, 703/836-6673.
- **Fairfax Seventh-Day Adventist Church**, 8950 Little River Turnpike, Fairfax, VA, 703/978-3386.
- **Fourth Street Friendship Seventh-Day Adventist Church**, 1611 4th Street NW, 202/797-9255.
- **Seventh-Day Adventist Church**, 727 W. Montgomery Avenue, Rockville, MD 301/424-4277.

Unitarian

- **Fairfax Unitarian Church**, 2709 Hunter Mill Road, Oakton, VA, 703/281-4230.
- **Unitarian-Universalist Church of Reston**, 1625 Wiehle Avenue, Reston, VA, 703/435-1180.
- **Universalist National Memorial Church**, 1810 16th Street NW, 202/387-3411.

Synagogues

Reform

- **Beth El Hebrew Congregation**, 3830 Seminary Road, Alexandria, VA, 703/370-9400.

- **Northern Virginia Hebrew Congregation**, 1441 Wiehle Avenue, Reston, VA, 703/437-7733.
- **Temple Beth Ami**, 800 Hurley Avenue, Rockville, MD, 301/340-6818.
- **Temple Emanuel**, 10101 Connecticut Avenue, Kensington, MD, 301/942-2000.
- **Temple Isaiah**, 5885 Robert Oliver Place, Columbia, MD, 301/596-0820.
- **Temple Micah**, 2829 Wisconsin Avenue NW, 202/342-9175.
- **Temple Rodef Shalom**, 2100 Westmoreland Street, Falls Church, VA, 703/532-2217.
- **Temple Sinai**, 3100 Military Road NW, 202/363-6394.
- **Washington Hebrew Congregation**, 3935 Macomb Street NW, 202/362-7100.

Conservative

- **Adas Israel Congregation**, Connecticut Avenue & Porter Street NW, 202/362-4433.
- **Agudas Achim Congregation Northern Virginia**, 2908 Valley Street, Alexandria, VA, 703/998-6460.
- **Arlington Fairfax Jewish Congregation**, 2920 Arlington Boulevard, Arlington, VA, 703/979-4466.
- **B'nai Israel Congregation**, 6301 Montrose Road, Rockville, MD, 301/881-6550.
- **Congregation Beth El of Montgomery County**, 8215 Old Georgetown Road, Bethesda, MD, 301/652-2606.
- **Congregation Olam Tikva**, 3800 Glenbrook Road, Fairfax, VA, 703/425-1880.
- **Mishkan Torah Reconstructionist Conservative**, 10 Ridge Road, Greenbelt, MD, 301/474-4223.
- **Ohr Kodesh Congregation**, 8402 Freyman Drive, Chevy Chase, MD, 301/589-3880.
- **Tifereth Israel Congregation**, 7701 16th Street NW, 202/882-1605.

Orthodox

- **Beth Sholom Congregation and Talmud Torah**, 11825 Seven Locks Road, Potomac, MD, 301/279-7010.
- **Congregation Ahavat Israel**, 9401 Mathy Drive, Fairfax, VA, 703/764-0239.
- **Georgetown Synagogue-Kesher Israel Congregation**, 2801 N Street NW, 202/337-2337.
- **Ohev Sholom Talmud Torah Congregation**, 7712 16th Street NW, 202/882-7225.
- **Southeast Hebrew Congregation**, 10900 Lockwood Drive, Silver Spring, MD, 301/593-2120.

Other Religions

Buddhist

- **Buddhist Congregational Church of America**, 5401 16th Street NW, 202/829-2423.
- **Buddhist Vihara Society Inc.**, 5017 16th Street NW, 202/723-0773.
- **Ekoji Buddhist Temple**, 8134 Old Keene Mill Road, Springfield, VA, 703/569-2311.
- **Nipponzan Myohoji Inc.**, 4900 16th Street NW, 202/291-2047.
- **Washington DC Buddhist Association**, 12733 Sesame Seed Court, Germantown, MD, 301/428-7936.
- **Won Buddhism of the America**, 8908 Potomac Station Lane, Potomac, MD, 301/983-9657.
- **Zen Buddhist Center of Washington DC Inc.**, 7004 9th Street NW, 202/829-1966.

Hare Krishna

- **International Society for Krishna Consciousness**, 10310 Oaklyn Drive, Potomac, MD, 301/299-2100.

Hindu

- **Golden Lotus Temple**, 4748 Western Avenue, Bethesda, MD, 301/229-3871.
- **Self Revelation Church of Absolute Monism**, 4748 Western Avenue, Bethesda, MD, 301/229-3871.

Islamic

- **Ahmadiyya Movement in Islam**, 15000 Good Hope Road, Silver Spring, MD 301/879-0110.
- **Islamic Education Center**, 7917 Montrose Road, Potomac, MD, 301/340-2070.
- **Masjid Muhammad**, 1519 4th Street NW, 202/483-8832.
- **Moorish Science Temple of America Number 71**, 732 Webster Street NW, 202/726-5025.
- **Mosque Emmanuel**, 12804 5th Street, Bowie, MD, 301/262-1146 and 5764 Georgia Avenue NW, 202/723-9619.
- **Muhammad's Mosque**, 1615-17 Kenilworth Avenue NE, 202/399-1010.

Gay & Lesbian Religious/Spiritual Groups

The Washington Blade runs a religion calendar listing all weekly events including all churches which welcome Washington's gay community. Below is a list of groups which hold weekly religious services:

- **Affirmation, United Methodists for Lesbian/Gay Concerns,** 703/866-6202
- **Bet Mishpachah Gay and Lesbian Synagogue of Washington, DC,** 202/833-1638
- **Dignity, Gay & Lesbian Catholics, Families and Friends,** 202/387-4516
- **Gay/Lesbian Unitarians,** 301/776-6891

W hether you want to help others who are less fortunate than yourself, save the world from environmental disasters, or make a few new friends, volunteering is the way to go. Just about every cause in the world has an office in Washington, so you should have little difficulty finding the perfect place to help out. Listed below are local volunteer information numbers, as well as the names of several respected organizations which are always looking for volunteer assistance.

- **Local Volunteer Information Offices**
- **Alexandria Volunteer Bureau**, 703/836-2176
- **Arlington County Volunteer Office**, 703/358-3222
- **DC Cares**, 202/289-7378
- **Fairfax County Volunteer Office**, 703/246-3460
- **Howard County Community Partnership for United Way**, 301/290-9392
- **Montgomery County Office of Volunteer Services**, 301/217-4949
- **Prince George's County Volunteer Action Center**, 301/779-9444

The Washington, DC Volunteer Guide, by Andrew Carroll, is available for $1 from DC Cares. *The Helping Handbook*, by Taisie Berkeley and Roger Newell, is available from the Greater-Washington Research Center (202/466-6680) for $5.

AIDS

- **Food & Friends**, 202/488-8278
- **Whitman Walker Clinic**, 202/797-3576

Alcohol

- **Alcoholics Anonymous**, 202/966-9115
- **Alcoholicos Anonimos de Habla Hispana**, 202/797-9738

Animals

- **Animal Rescue of Montgomery County, MD**, 301/279-1823
- **Animal Welfare League of Arlington County, VA**, 703/931-9241
- **Washington Humane Society**, 202/333-4010

Children/Youth Services

- **Boys and Girls Clubs of Greater Washington**, 301/587-4315
- **Boys and Girls Homes of Maryland**, 301/589-8444
- **Children's Defense Fund**, 202/628-8787
- **Court Appointed Special Advocates**, 202/328-2191
- **Higher Achievement Program**, 202/842-5116
- **Outreach for Parent Teens**, 703/358-5819
- **Sasha Bruce Youthwork**, 202/547-7777

Culture & the Arts

- **Business Volunteers for the Arts**, 202/638-2406
- **Friends of the Kennedy Center**, 202/416-8000
- **Friends of the National Zoo**, 202/673-4955
- **Smithsonian Institution**, 202/357-2700

Disabled

- **Columbia Lighthouse for the Blind**, 202/462-2900 ext. 3045
- **Disabled American Veterans**, 202/554-3501
- **Jewish Foundation for Group Homes**, 301/984-3839
- **Metropolitan Washington Ear**, 301/681-6636
- **National Center for Therapeutic Riding**, 202/362-4537
- **Recording for the Blind**, 202/244-8990
- **Special Olympics**, 202/544-7770; 301/738-7805; 703/719-0040

Elderly

- **Iona Senior Services**, 202/966-1055
- **Goodwin House**, 703/824-1357
- **Meals on Wheels**, 202/723-5617

Environment

- **Arlingtonians for a Clean Environment**, 703/358-6427
- **Garden Resources of Washington (GROW)**, 202/234-0591
- **National Park Service**, 202/619-7077
- **Patuxent Environmental Science Center**, 301/497-5833
- **Sierra Club**, 202/547-2326

Gay & Lesbian

- **Gay & Lesbian Activists Alliance**, 202/667-5139
- **Gay & Lesbian Hotline**, 202/833-3234

Health

- **American Cancer Society**, 202/483-2600
- **American Red Cross**, blood drives, 202/737-8300
- **Hospital for Sick Children**, 202/832-4400
- **National Rehabilitation Hospital**, 202/877-1000

Hungry & Homeless

- **Habitat for Humanity**, 202/563-3411; 301/762-3437
- **Hand to Hand**, 301/983-HAND
- **Martha's Table**, 202/328-6608
- **So Others Might Eat**, 202/581-8000

International

- **Ayuda Legal Aid**, 202/387-4848
- **Central American Refugee Center**, 202/328-9799
- **Latin American Youth Center**, 202/483-1140
- **Spanish Education Development Center**, 202/462-8405
- **Youth for Understanding**, 202/966-6800

Legal

- **American Civil Liberties Union (ACLU)**, 202/544-1681
- **Legal Aid Society of DC**, 202/628-1161
- **Legal Council for the Elderly**, 202/434-2170

Literacy

- **Literacy Volunteers of America**, 202/387-1772
- **Washington Literacy Council**, 202/387-9029
- **Push Literacy Action Now**, 202/547-8903

Women

- **National Organization for Women**, 202/331-0066
- **My Sister's Place**, 202/529-5991

Other

- **Catholic Charities**, 703/841-2531
- **DC Jewish Community Center**, 202/775-1765
- **Lutheran Social Services**, 202/232-6380
- **Salvation Army**, 202/829-0100
- **United Jewish Appeal**, 301/230-7200
- **Washington National Cathedral**, 202/537-8990
- **Washington Urban League**, 202/829-7334
- **YMCA**, 202/232-6700
- **YWCA**, 202/626-0700

Many newcomers arrive in Washington to work before they have a chance to find a permanent home. And because the city attracts tourists in droves, lodgings are not hard to find here — unless you arrive during a presidential inauguration. While there are no great deals on lodging in the Washington area, penny-pinchers can find places to stay throughout the town, especially at some of the more well-known, low-priced hotels. You can call the hotels yourself, or call **1-800-VISIT-DC**, a service that will reserve a room for you, often at a discounted rate.

Hotels

Inexpensive Hotels

- **Days Inns**, 9137 Baltimore Boulevard, College Park, 301/345-5000; 4400 Connecticut Avenue NW, 202/244-5600; 2000 Jefferson Davis Highway, Arlington, 703/920-8600. Nationally, call 800/DAYSINN.
- **EconoLodges**, 18715 North Frederick Avenue, Gaithersburg, 301/963-3840; 6800 Lee Highway, Arlington, 703/538-5300.

Middle-priced Hotels

- **Embassy Suites Hotels**, 1900 Diagonal Road, Alexandria, 703/684-5900; 1250 22nd Street NW, 202/857-3388; 4300 Military Road NW, 202/362-9300.
- **Marriot Hotels**, 5151 Pooks Hill Road, Bethesda, 301/897-9400; 1331 Pennsylvania Avenue NW, 202/393-2000; 8028 Leesburg Pike, Vienna, 703/734-3200.

Luxury Hotels

- **Four Season Hotel**, 2800 Pennsylvania Avenue NW, 202/342-0444.
- **Hay-Adams Hotel**, One Lafayette Square NW, 202/638-6600.
- **Ritz-Carlton Hotel**, 2100 Massachusetts Avenue NW, 202/293-2100.
- **Willard Inter-Continental Hotel**, 1401 Pennsylvania Avenue NW, 202/628-9100.

Bed & Breakfasts

Call the **Bed & Breakfast League** at **202/363-7767** or the **Bed & Breakfast Reservation Service** at **202/328-3510** for information on inns both in and out of the Washington area. Or you might want to try one of the following:

- **Embassy Inn**, 1627 16th Street NW, 202/234-7800.
- **Hereford House**, 604 South Carolina Avenue SE, 202/543-0102.
- **Kalorama Guest House**, 1854 Mintwood Place NW, 202/667-6369.
- **Windsor Inn**, 1842 16th Street NW, 202/667-0300.

Hostels

- **American Youth Hostels National Office**, 733 15th Street NW, 202/783-6161.
- **Bear's Den AYH Hostel**, Route 1, Box 288, Bluemont, 540/554-8708.
- **Potomac Area AYH Hostel**, 1017 K Street NW, 202/783-4943.

Summer Housing

Several local universities rent out their dorm rooms to non-students as well as students during the summer. These rooms are furnished with such basics as a bed, desk, and dresser. You will most likely have to share a bathroom with others. A few rooms even come with air conditioning, practically a necessity for those who don't consider perspiration a hobby.

Different universities have different rent agreements. George Washington University, for example, charges per night, regardless of how long you stay — so it gets pretty expensive if you have a room to yourself and stay for more than a month, but is really convenient if you need a place for two weeks. Here's a list of colleges and phone numbers:

- **American University,** 4400 Massachusetts Avenue NW. Call the Office of Residential Life at 202/885-3370.
- **Georgetown University,** 37th & O Streets NW. Call Housing Services at 202/687-4560.
- **George Washington University,** 2121 Eye Street NW. Call the Residential Living Office at 202/994-6688.
- **University of Maryland,** Baltimore Boulevard, College Park, MD. Call the Department of Resident Life at 301/314-2100.

January

Martin Luther King's Birthday Observance, Lincoln Memorial

February

Chinese New Year Parade, Chinatown, 202/724-4091
Abraham Lincoln's Birthday Observance Concert,
Lincoln Memorial
George Washington's Birthday Parade, Old Town Alexandria,
703/838-4200
George Washington's Birthday Celebration, Washington Monument
Black History Month Exhibition, Smithsonian Institution,
202/357-2700, Martin Luther King Memorial Library, 202/727-1211

March

Maple Syrup Festival, Cunningham Falls State Park in Thurmont,
MD, 301/271-7574
Alexandria St. Patrick's Day Parade, Old Town Alexandria
Washington St. Patrick's Day Parade, Constitution Avenue,
202/673-7660

April

National Cherry Blossom Festival & Parade, Constitution Avenue
White House Easter Egg Roll, White House, 202/456-2200
Smithsonian Kite Festival, Washington Monument grounds,
202/357-3030
International Film Fest DC, at various area theaters, 202/724-5613
Goddard Space Flight Center Community Day, Goddard Space
Center, Greenbelt, MD, 301/286-2000
White House Spring Garden Tours, 202/456-2200

May

Annapolis Waterfront Arts Festival, Annapolis Harbor
Virginia Gold Cup, The Plains, VA
School Safety Patrol Parade, Constitution Avenue
Chesapeake Bay Bridge Walk, Chesapeake Bay Bridge
Andrews Air Force Base Air Show, Andrews AFB, Camp Springs, MD, 301/981-1110
Preakness Celebration, Pimlico Raceway, Baltimore, MD, 410/542-9400
Memorial Day Ceremonies, at various area memorials
Memorial Day Weekend Concert, West Lawn, U.S. Capitol, 202/619-7222

June

Kemper Open, Tournament Players Club, at Avenel in Potomac, MD, 301/469-3737
Capital Jazz Fest, Nissan Pavilion in Manassass, VA
Shakespeare Theater Free-for-all, Carter Barron Amphitheater
U.S. Open, Congressional Country Club
Alexandria Red Cross Waterfront Festival, City Marina, Alexandria, VA, 703/549-8300
Wolf Trap Jazz & Blues Festival, Wolf Trap, Vienna, VA, 703/255-1800
Festival of American Folklife, the mall

July

Festival of American Folklife, the mall, 202/357-2700
Fourth of July Celebration, the mall, 202/619-7222
Legg-Mason Tennis Classic, William H.G. FitzGerald Tennis Center
Bastille Day Waiters Races, Pennsylvania Avenue
Chincoteague Pony Swim, Chincoteague Island, MD

August

Flying Circus Hot Air Balloon Festival, Flying Circus Airport in Bealeton, VA
Georgia Avenue Day, Banneker Park, 202/723-5166
Maryland Renaissance Festival, Crownsville, MD
National Frisbee Festival, Washington Monument

September

Maryland Seafood Festival, Sandy Point State Park, MD
Adams Morgan Day, Columbia Road, 202/332-3292

October

German-American Day, Union Station, 202/554-2664
Fells Point Fun Festival, Baltimore, MD
Apple Butter Festival, Berkeley Springs, WV
Taste of DC, Pennsylvania Avenue, 202/724-4093
International Gold Cup Steeplechase Races, the Plains, VA
Marine Corps Marathon, throughout Washington and VA
Columbus Day Ceremonies, Union Station, 202/619-7222
White House Fall Garden Tours, South Lawn, 202/456-2200

November

Veterans' Day, ceremonies at various locations
Waterfowl Festival, Easton, MD
Marine Corps Marathon, Iwo Jima Memorial, 703/690-3431

December

Scottish Christmas Walk, Alexandria, VA
White House Christmas Tours, the White House
New Year's Eve Celebrations,
various city governments offer events
National Christmas Tree Lighting
U.S. Botanic Garden's Christmas Poinsettia Show, 202/226-4082

* Indicates that an area code is not necessary in all the District, Maryland, or Virginia.

Aging

Alexandria Aging Assistance Information & Referral 703/838-0920
American Association of Retired Persons (AARP) 202/434-2277
Arlington Area Agency on Aging .703/358-5030
District Office on Aging Information & Referral 202/724-5626
Fairfax County Area Agency on Aging 703/246-5411
Montgomery County Office on Aging Information &
Family Resources 301/468-4443
Prince George's County Bureau of Aging 301/699-2680
Senior Citizen's Counseling and Delivery Services 202/678-2800

Alcohol & Drug Abuse

Alexandria Alcoholism & Drug Abuse Treatment 703/329-2000
Arlington Alcohol Safety & Action Program (ASAP) 703/358-4420
District Alcohol & Drug Hotline 800/888-9383
Fairfax County Substance Abuse Services 703/359-7040
Montgomery County Adolescent Addiction Program 301/217-1375
Montgomery County Adult Addiction Programs 301/217-1680
Narcotics Anonymous 301/662-3263

Animals

Alexandria Animal Shelter 703/838-4775
Animal Welfare League of Alexandria 703/838-4774
Arlington County Animal Welfare League 703/931-9241
District Animal Control Shelter .202/576-6664
Fairfax County Animal Control .703/830-3310
Fairfax County Animal Shelter .703/830-1100
Montgomery County Animal Rescue 301/279-1823
Montgomery County Animal Shelter 301/217-6999
Prince George's County Animal Control 301/499-8300

Automobiles

American Automobile Association (AAA) 703/222-6000
District Department of Motor Vehicles 202/727-6680
District Booted Vehicles 202/727-5000
District Abandoned Vehicle Removal 202/645-4227
Maryland Motor Vehicles Administration 301/948-3177
Virginia Department of Motor Vehicles 703/761-4655

Child Abuse

Alexandria Child Abuse & Neglect Complaints 703/838-0800
Arlington County Child Protective Services 703/358-5100
District Child Abuse & Neglect Hotline 202/727-0995
Fairfax County Child Abuse Complaints 703/246-7400
Montgomery County Child Abuse & Neglect Complaints . .301/217-4417
Prince George's County Child Abuse & Neglect Hotline . . .301/699-8605

Consumer Complaints & Services

Alexandria Office of Consumer Affairs 703/838-4350
Arlington County Office of Consumer Affairs 703/358-3260
Better Business Bureau 202/393-8000
District Consumer Complaints 202/727-7080
Fairfax County Consumer Affairs Office 703/222-8435
Montgomery County Consumer Affairs Office 301/217-7373
Prince George's County Office of Citizen's
and Consumer Affairs 301/952-4700
Washington Consumers' Checkbook 202/347-7283

Crime

Crime Solvers .800/673-2777 or 202/393-2222

Discrimination

Arlington County Human Rights-EEO Office 703/358-3929
District Discrimination Complaint Intake Unit 202/939-8740
Fairfax County Human Rights Commission 703/324-2953
Montgomery County Human Relations Commission 301/468-4260
Prince George's County Human Relations Commission . . .301/952-3408

Fire, Emergency Number *911

Health & Medical Care

AIDS Hotline 202/332-AIDS
HIV Testing 202/332-3926
Lead Poisoning Prevention Program 202/727-9850
VD Hotline 202/832-7000
Poison Control Center 202/625-3333

Legal Referral

District Bar Association 202/626-3499
Montgomery County Bar Association 301/279-9100
Virginia Bar Association, ...800/552-7977

Local Government Information

Alexandria 703/838-4000
Arlington County 703/358-3000
District 202/727-1000
Fairfax County 703/246-2000
Montgomery County 301/217-6500
Prince George's County 301/350-9700

Marriage Licenses

Alexandria Circuit Court, ...703/838-5046
Arlington County Circuit Court 703/358-4510
District Superior Court Marriage Bureau, ...202/879-4840
Fairfax County Judicial Center 703/246-2993
Montgomery County Circuit Court License Department . . .301/217-7075
Price George's County Circuit Court License Department .301/952-3288

Police, Emergency Number *911

Public Schools Information

Alexandria 703/824-6600
Arlington County 703/358-6000
District, ...202/724-4289
Fairfax County 703/246-2502
Montgomery County 301/279-3391
Prince George's County 301/952-6000

Rape & Sexual Assault

Alexandria 703/683-7273
Arlington County 703/358-4848
District Rape Crisis Center 202/333-7273
Fairfax County 703/ 360-7273
Montgomery County 301/217-1355
Prince George's County 301/618-3154

Sanitation & Garbage

Alexandria Refuse Collection & Sanitation 703/751-5130
Arlington County Refuse Removal 703/358-6570
District Trash Collection 202/645-7044
Fairfax County Refuse Collection Service 703/631-1484
Montgomery County Refuse & Recycling Collection 301/217-2410
Prince George's County Refuse Collection & Complaints .301/952-4750

Street Maintenance

Alexandria, Transportation Construction & Inspection 703/838-4966
Arlington County Public Works Operations & Inspections .703/358-3576
District Public Works Pothole Maintenance 202/767-8527
Fairfax County Public Works Road Management 703/324-2000
Montgomery County Highway Maintenance &
Road Repair 301/217-2159
Prince George's County Highway Maintenance
Central Services 301/499-8520

Time *844-1212

Tourism & Travel

National Park Service Information 202/619-7222
Visitor Information Center 202/789-7000

Transportation

Airports:
Baltimore Washington
International Airport . . . . .410/859-7111 or 301/261-1000
Dulles International Airport 703/661-2700
National Airport 703/419-8000
Buses:
Alexandria DASH 703/370-DASH
Fairfax Connector 703/339-7200
MetroBus 202/637-7000
Ride On 301/217-7433
Subway:
Metrorail 202/637-7000
Trains:
Amtrak 800-USA-RAIL
Maryland Rail Commuter (MARC) 800/325-RAIL
Virginia Railway Express 703/497-7777

Utility Emergencies

PEPCO 202/833-7500
Virginia Power 202/833-1982
Washington Gas 703/750-1400
Washington Suburban Sanitary Commission 301/206-4002

Voter Information

Alexandria 703/838-4050
Arlington County 703/358-3456
District 202/727-2525
Fairfax County 703/222-0776

League of Women Voters 202/429-1965
Montgomery County 301/217-8683
Prince George's County 301/627-2814

Weather *936-1212

Adams Morgan 8, 12, 19, 20, 22, 92
Airports 51, 84, 140
Alexandria 8, 12, 40, 44, 45
American University Park 12, 26
Animals Numbers (See also, Pets) 128, 137
Annapolis 39, 40
Antique Districts 92
Apartment & Home Guides 53
Apartment Hunting 51
Apartment Finding Services 54, 55
Appliances 87
Arlington 8, 10, 12, 41, 42, 44
Art Museums 99, 100
Au Pairs 79
Automobiles Numbers 138

Baby sitting 78
Ballet 96
Ballston 12, 44
Baltimore Washington International Airport 84, 140
Banking 67, 68
Baseball 109
Basketball 109, 111, 112
Bed & Breakfast 132
Beds & Bedding 88
Bell Atlantic Telephone 58
Bethesda 8, 12, 13, 29, 30, 31, 32, 35
Bicycling 112
Blues 97
Boating 112, 113
Bookstores 88, 89
Buses 82, 140

C&O Canal Towpath 105, 112

Cable Television 60
Capitol Hill 12, 27
Car Rental 84
Carpool Services 73, 82
Checking Accounts 68
Chevy Chase 8, 12, 23, 29, 35
Child Abuse Numbers 138
Child Care 77
Choruses 96, 97
Churches 79, 119
Classifieds 53
Cleveland Park 12, 23, 24, 25
Clubs 97, 98, 101
Colleges 103, 104, 132
Columbia 33, 38, 39
Columbia Heights 20
Comedy Clubs 99
Computers 89, 90
Concert Venues 97
Connecticut Avenue Corridor 23
Consumer Complaints Numbers 138
Consumer Services 64, 73, 87, 138
Credit Cards 69, 70
Crime 10, 20, 27, 35, 45, 138
Crystal City 12, 43, 44
Cultural Life 95
Culture for Kids 101, 102
Curling 113

Dance 97
Darnestown 32
Department of Parks and Recreation 107, 111, 116, 117
Department Stores 69, 70, 85, 87
Diaper Services 73
Dinner Theaters 99
Discrimination Numbers 138
Driver's Licenses 58
Dry Cleaning 73
Dulles International Airport 13, 48, 51, 84, 140
Dupont Circle 12, 18, 19, 22, 26

East Potomac Park 105
Electricity 57
Emergency Baby sitting 78

Fairlington 41
Fishing 113
Foggy Bottom 12, 16, 17

Food Delivery .... .73
Football .... .110, 111
Foreign Currency Exchange .... .74
Friendship Heights .... .29
Frisbee .... .113
Furniture .... .90
Furniture Rental .... .74

Gaithersburg .... .33
Garden Centers .... .91, 92
Gas .... .57
Gay & Lesbian Religious/Spiritual Groups .... .124
Georgetown .... .12, 15, 16, 17, 40, 43, 92
Getting Settled .... .57
Golf .... .113
Government Numbers .... .138, 139, 140
Great Falls .... .12, 46, 106, 114, 115
Green Space .... .10, 105, 106, 107

Handicapped Services .... .75, 76, 128
Hardware .... .91
Health & Medical Care Numbers .... .129, 138
Health Clubs .... .116
Helpful Services .... .73
Higher Education .... .103, 104
Hiking .... .113
Hockey .... .110
Horse Racing .... .110
Horseback Riding .... .114
Hostels .... .132
Hotels .... .131
House Cleaning .... .74
House Hunting .... .51, 52, 53, 54
Housewares .... .91

Ice Skating .... .114
In-line Skating .... .114
Income Taxes .... .70, 71
Insurance .... .56
Introduction 7

Jazz .... .97

Kalorama .... .12, 22
Kentlands .... .33

Laurel .... .36, 37
Landlord Issues .... .56

Lansburgh 27
Lawn Care 74

Leases 55
Legal Referral Numbers 139
Local Government Information Numbers .139
Lodgings 131
Loudoun County 48

Mail Receiving Services 75
Market Square 27
Marriage License Numbers 139
Mattresses 88
McLean 12, 46
Mitchellville 38
Money Matters 67
Montgomery Village 33
Mount Pleasant 8, 10, 20
Movie Theaters (Art, Revival, Non-Major Studio Releases) 101
Ms. Utility Locating Service 58
Museums, Art 24, 99, 100
Museums, Other .43, 100, 101, 102, 103
Music, Classical 96
Music, Contemporary 97

Nannies 77, 78
National Airport 12, 43, 84, 140
National Mall 105
Neighborhoods 13
New U 21
Newspaper Classified Advertising 53
Newspaper Subscriptions 62, 63

On-line Resources 53
On-line Services 64, 65
Opera 96
Outlet Shopping 93

PEPCO 9, 57, 140
Package Delivery 75
Parkfairfax 45
Parking Laws 9, 20, 59, 60
Passport Services 62
Pet Laws 63
Pet Services 63, 64, 75
Phone Service 58
Places of Worship 119
Polo 115

Potomac 10, 15, 31, 45, 46
Potomac Electric Power Company 9, 57
Public Schools Numbers 139

Radio 61
Rape & Sexual Assault Numbers 139
Real Estate Brokers 54
Recycling 62
Rent Control 52, 56
Reston 12, 33, 47
Rock Creek Park 8, 10, 22, 24, 105, 112, 114
Rockville 12, 31, 32
Roommate Referral Services 55
Rosslyn 12, 43, 44
Running 115

Sailing 112, 113
Sanitation & Garbage Numbers 139
Savage 37
Savings Accounts 68
Security Deposits 55
Services for People with Disabilities 75
Shaw 21
Shopping for the Home 85
Soccer 110, 115, 117
Sports 109
Sports, College 111
Sports for Kids 117
Sports, Participatory 111
Sports, Professional 109
Storage Spaces 75
Street Maintenance Numbers 140
Subway 81, 140
Summer Housing 132
Swimming 115
Synagogues 79, 122

Takoma Park 12, 34, 56
Taxes 70, 71
Taxis 83
Television 60, 61
Temporary Lodgings 131, 132
Tennis 116
Theaters 98, 101
Theaters, Community 41, 98, 99
Theaters for Kids 102
Theater, Professional 98
Tourism Numbers 140

Trains .... .82, 140
Transportation .... .81, 140
Transportation Numbers 140

Union Station .... .27
Universities .... .78, 103, 104, 132
University Park .... .12, 35, 36
Useful Telephone Numbers 137
Utility Emergency Numbers 140

Van Ness .... .23, 24
Vehicle Registration .... .58, 59
Virginia Power .... .57
Visitor Information (See Tourism Numbers) 140
Volunteering .... .127
Voter Information Numbers 140
Voter Registration .... .61

Warehouse Shopping .... .93
Washington D.C. Area Year 133
Washington Gas .... .57
Washington Harbor Complex .... .15
West Potomac Park 105
Windsurfing .... .112, 113
Woodley Park 23, 24

Yard Sales .... .94

Jeremy L. Milk is a product of the nation's capital. He grew up just outside the city and has stayed in the area except for a few years spent in Asia. He has written for *The Chronicle of Higher Education*, *The Washingtonian* magazine, and the *American Legion*, and now works as a Washington correspondent for Japan's largest daily newspaper.

Leslie Milk is the Lifestyle Editor at *The Washingtonian* magazine and the winner of the 1994 gold medal for investigative reporting from the City and Regional Magazine Association. A transplanted New Yorker who arrived here before the first real bagel baker, she has lived here through the administrations of six presidents. Milk is a former columnist for *The Washington Post* and the *Journal* newspapers. She is also a playwright.

THE ORIGINAL, ALWAYS UPDATED, ABSOLUTELY INVALUABLE GUIDES FOR PEOPLE MOVING TO A CITY!

Find out about neigborhoods, apartment hunting, money matters, deposits/leases, getting settled, helpful services, shopping for the home, places of worship, belonging, sports/recreation, volunteering, green space, transportation, temporary lodgings and useful telephone numbers!

	# COPIES	TOTAL
Newcomer's Handbook™ for Atlanta	_____ x $13.95	$_____
Newcomer's Handbook™ for Boston	_____ x $13.95	$_____
Newcomer's Handbook™ for Chicago	_____ x $13.95	$_____
Newcomer's Handbook™ for Los Angeles	_____ x $13.95	$_____
Newcomer's Handbook™ for Minneapolis-St. Paul	_____ x $14.95	$_____
Newcomer's Handbook™ for New York City	_____ x $16.95	$_____
Newcomer's Handbook™ for San Francisco	_____ x $13.95	$_____
Newcomer's Handbook™ for Washington, DC	_____ x $13.95	$_____

SUBTOTAL $_____

TAX (IL residents add 8.75% sales tax) $_____

POSTAGE & HANDLING ($5.00 first book, $.75 each add'l) $_____

TOTAL $_____

SHIP TO:

_____
Name

_____
Title

_____
Company

_____
Address

_____ _____ _____
City   State   Zip

_____
Phone Number

FIRST BOOKS

Send this order form and a check or money order payable to: First Books, Inc.

First Books, Inc., Mail Order Department
P.O. Box 578147, Chicago, IL 60657
773-276-5911

Allow 2-3 weeks for delivery.

DO YOU THINK YOU KNOW THE WASHINGTON, DC AREA BETTER THAN WE DO? TELL US!

If you are the first to offer any new information about
Washington, DC that is subsequently used in the next
Newcomer's Handbook™ for Washington, DC,
we'll send you a free copy of our next edition.

SUGGESTIONS:

_____

_____

_____

_____

_____

YOUR NAME: _____

YOUR ADDRESS (PLEASE INCLUDE YOUR TELEPHONE NUMBER): _____

_____

_____

Help keep this guide current. If a listing has changed, let us know.

UPDATES: _____

_____

_____

_____

_____

Send to: First Books, Inc.
P.O. Box 578147, Chicago, IL 60657

Smart Business Travel

HOW TO STAY SAFE WHEN YOU'RE ON THE ROAD

Don't be scared, be prepared!

"Offers great safety tips for the business traveler." – *Chicago Tribune*

"Handy"– *Frequent Flyer*

"Contains plenty of common sense"– *Los Angeles Times*

"Recommended"– *Houston Chronicle*

	# COPIES		TOTAL
Smart Business Travel	_____	× $12.95	$_____
TAX (IL residents add 8.75% sales tax)			$_____
POSTAGE & HANDLING ($3.00 first book, $.75 each add'l)			$_____
TOTAL			$_____

SHIP TO:

_____
Name

_____
Title

_____
Company

_____
Address

_____
City   State   Zip

_____
Phone Number

Send this order form and a check or money order
payable to First Books, Inc.

First Books, Inc. Mail Order Department
P.O. Box 578147, Chicago, IL 60657
773-276-5911

Allow 2-3 weeks for delivery.

Visit our web site at
http://www.firstbooks.com
for a sample of all our books.